BODY & SOUL

A Married Couple's Guide
to Discovering and Understanding Our
Unique Sexual Personalities

Body & Soul

Duane Storey &
Sanford Kulkin
with Mary Ann Mayo

MULTNOMAH BOOKS • SISTERS, OREGON

BODY AND SOUL
published by Multnomah Books
a part of the Questar publishing family

International Standard Book Number: 0-88070-742-9

Cover design by Bruce DeRoos

Printed in the United States of America

For information:
QUESTAR PUBLISHERS, INC.
POST OFFICE BOX 1720
SISTERS, OREGON 97759

95 96 97 98 99 00 01 02 — 10 9 8 7 6 5 4 3 2

TABLE OF CONTENTS

PART I

Personality and Sexuality:

Designed for Intimacy

INTRODUCTION TO PART I

Next to your relationship with Jesus Christ, the most intimate relationship you can have is with your spouse. When true intimacy develops, marriage becomes a rich, fulfilling experience.

Your efforts to develop an intimate marriage are enhanced when you increase your knowledge of how marriage works. The first eight chapters of this book will help you do just that, by providing you with a fuller understanding of personality styles (using the respected DISC personality assessment system) and gender differences, which, taken together, help determine our sexual styles—our *sexual personalities*.

I am sometimes asked, "Is all this personality stuff more of that modern pop psychology?" The answer is, no. First of all, studies of personality are based on observation, and have been done for centuries. As far back as Hippocrates we see the development of four basic personality types—Choleric, Sanguine, Phlegmatic, and Melancholy. For millennia, scholars have been adding to and refining what is known about personality types so that, today, we have a good understanding of how the different personality styles respond to various life situations, and how they can mesh...or clash...with each other.

The material presented in the following chapters is both biblical and practical. It isn't meant to replace Scripture as the primary source of information about marital intimacy; the principles supplied are merely tools which can help you to understand yourself and your spouse better.

Can the kind of information contained in this book really improve your marriage? My answer is simply, "Yes, it can...if you work at it." By possessing the tools presented here and committing to use them to develop intimacy in your marriage, while at the same time entrusting God's Spirit to empower you, there is the wonderful possibility of entering into a new dimension of intimacy with your spouse—*Body and Soul*.

—Duane Storey

CHAPTER ONE

Restoring Eden

"Mommmm, where's my homework?" Katherine's plaintive wail made its way into the bedroom where Evelyn Summers was putting the finishing touches on her mascara.

"I'll be right there to help you look, honey," she responded, trying not to be annoyed.

Once Katherine's homework was found, Evelyn walked her daughter and her husband, Allen, to the car. Allen always dropped Katherine off at her elementary school on his way to work, while Evelyn drove Timmy to his kindergarten class half an hour later. At night they reversed the order as they performed the ritual tucking-in ceremony. Each parent enjoyed these special times with the two children.

Allen made sure Katherine buckled up, he closed the car door carefully, then he walked over to Evelyn who was now clearing toys and dog dishes off the back porch. "Any hitches in our plans for tonight?" he asked quietly.

Evelyn let out a little laugh, "No, I think tonight is going to work—no signs of chicken pox or visiting relatives yet."

"Good," Allen said with a smile. "I'll try to be home a little early so I can help get the kids ready."

"Oh, I *know* why you want to come home early," Evelyn teased. Allen laughed and turned back toward the car.

Evelyn deeply appreciated Allen's involvement with the children. Normally, both parents pitched in during the evening hours to "take care of business," so they could finally sit down together, visit, watch TV, or work on a mutual project.

Tonight, however, was special. Once a month, Allen and Evelyn left their kids for the evening with their friends, the Thornbergs—who expected the favor to be returned with their two children. The first few times, the Summers had simply gone out to dinner. But lately, they had delighted in planning a private evening at home.

Allen called at midday to remind his wife that he loved her and, "Tonight we're going to be alone, remember?" Of course she hadn't forgotten. On her way home from work, Evelyn picked up some nice prawns at the fish market and a still-warm loaf of bread at the bakery next door. She was only half surprised when Allen walked in with fresh flowers.

Once the kids were safely at the Thornbergs, the Summers shared a leisurely dinner and slowly moved into their private world. After cleaning up, while Evelyn lit some new candles, Allen prepared a bubble bath for the two of them. As the candlelight flickered on the ceiling, their lovemaking progressed.

Making love actually had begun for Allen and Evelyn twelve hours earlier with their chat on the back porch. It had been nurtured by Allen's phone call. Both husband and wife had allowed themselves to anticipate the evening throughout the day. And now that the time had come, they were prepared to be intimate, both emotionally and physically.

SEX—A MARITAL CHALLENGE

Just about everyone agrees that making love can be wonderful. And people like Evelyn and Allen Summers have learned to make the most of it—to celebrate and delight in it. But nearly everyone also agrees sex can be challenging. More specifically, having a satisfying sexual relationship is often difficult. Wise couples—like the Summers—have learned to work at it. And they believe it is well worth the effort.

Of course, we aren't always given accurate information by our culture. In the movies, pleasurable lovemaking seems so easy. Two people meet, fall in love, and either dive or drift into peak sexual experiences filled with passion, creativity, and freshness. Unfortunately, reality seldom resembles the fantasies depicted in films, books, and legends. In real life, even when there is genuine love, strong motivation, compatible personalities, passable bodies, and marriages sanctified by God—sex is often difficult.

It wasn't meant to be that way at the beginning. It's just that a few things have come between good satisfying sexual relationships and the men and women trying to have them—things like living in a fallen world that hardly resembles the Garden of Eden; guilt; ignorance; unrealistic expectations; and a virtual war between the sexes. It hasn't helped that men and women are reluctant to talk to one another about their sexual needs, wants, or likes—at least in ways that can be clearly heard.

More by accident than design, lovemaking occasionally goes right, providing a glimpse of what is supposed to be. But the surprised participants are often too unsure of what worked in order to make it happen again, so subsequent sex falls short of its potential. It remains, too often, a source of frustration, pain, and plain old embarrassment.

SEARCHING FOR SOLUTIONS

Some people go to great lengths to improve their sexual satisfaction. Certain individuals seem to think that airing their problems on daytime television is an option. There are those who check into clinics specializing in treatment of sexual problems. Still others obtain the services of a good therapist, physician, or pastor—certainly the most reasonable solution when professional help is a practical alternative.

Unfortunately, the most common response to sexual difficulties is to muddle along, trying to make the best of something that could be far better. That's what most people do. But the fact that you have picked up a book on sexual personalities indicates that you want more for yourself, your marriage, and your mate.

KEYS FOR IMPROVING SEX

This book is fashioned to help you understand your sexual behavior—why you respond the way you do and why your partner responds the way he or she does. As you consider the pages that follow, we hope you and your spouse will learn to communicate more effectively, based on your understanding of your individual personalities. If so, you will enter a new world of expanding intimacy.

It is legitimate to ask, "If sex is the problem, why is understanding personality a solution?" The truth is, sex is more than two bodies coupling. Sexual encounters are laden with meaning and significance beyond the tangible. Lasting sexual satisfaction requires connections that are both emotional and physical.

The very desire to enrich or improve our love lives is a precursor to improvement. Such an attitude sets the stage for changes to take place. Studies show that both marital counseling and sexual therapy result in increased sexual satisfaction. In other words, you don't always have to talk about sex to make things better—but you do have to talk.

Sexual improvement occurs for three reasons:

1. A couple's commitment to sexual enrichment.

2. Improved communication, which leads to…

3. Increased intimacy.

If there is any magic ingredient to a healthy sex life, it is *intimacy*.

The good news is that for most readers, improvement can be experienced in the privacy of your home with your spouse. Our goal in writing this book is to help you in two specific ways.

- **You will learn how your personality and your partner's affect the way you talk about and approach sex.**
- **You will discover how to use that knowledge to increase your level of intimacy.**

We hope you will read and discuss this book as a couple. You may even want to read it aloud to one another. But don't despair if your partner lacks interest; even the things you learn alone will improve communication.

HAVE WE DISCOVERED A MAGIC FORMULA?

We Americans love the quick fix. We say to the physician, "Give me a pill, but don't ask me to change my lifestyle, Doc!" We instruct our therapist, "Fix my spouse!" We bargain with God, "If You love me, Lord, make life easier. Then I'll straighten up."

Whether we're concerned with physical, emotional, spiritual or sexual issues, there are no instant formulas. Improvement calls for commitment, patience, knowledge, honesty, and willingness to make things better. *Body and Soul: Understanding Your Sexual Personality* is a tool to make the task easier. It greatly increases the likelihood of your sexual relationship being enriched.

Author Duane L. Storey is founder of Resources for Communication Concepts in Sisters, Oregon, where he serves as behavioral consultant. He also serves as an interim pastor. Duane brings to you the riches of wisdom he has gained in twenty-five years of pastoring and counseling. His experience provides him with a remarkable depth of understanding of marriage and the interaction between different types of personalities.

Co-author Sanford G. (Sandy) Kulkin, a highly sought-after consultant and lecturer, is an expert in behavioral "styles." He specializes in teaching how an understanding of those styles can help people communicate better and work together more effectively. Sandy's expertise with the DISC model will put you in touch with your spouse's strengths and weaknesses, as well as your own.

Besides co-authoring this book, Mary Ann Mayo has written several others regarding sexual therapy, sex education for children and teens, body image, and women's mental, physical, and spiritual health. Mary Ann is a licensed marriage, family, and child counselor in California. She has a private practice where she is involved in patient education programs with her Ob./Gyn. physician husband of more than thirty-one years. She and Dr. Mayo often speak together on sexuality in marriage.

WHAT MAKES LOVEMAKING PLEASURABLE?

We all agree that sex is not the most important aspect of the marriage relationship. Yet it comes as little surprise that married couples who have unsatisfactory sex lives are less likely to feel good about other aspects of their marriage. Sex may play a small role in everyday living, but when it goes wrong, pain radiates everywhere. Most people would go so far as to say that a good sex life is essential to a happy marriage.

You may be surprised to learn what research literature says about sex and spirituality: The couples most satisfied with the sexual intimacy level in their marriages share a common spiritual base. Contrary to the prevailing stereotype, religious people may be the most sexually satisfied folks around! Clearly, sensitivity to the spiritual aspects of life does not keep one from appreciating the sensuous components of sex. The Janus Report, a 1993 update of the sexual practices of Americans, reiterates that religious men and women are the ones most satisfied with their sexual and marital relationships. It also reports a positive correlation between being religious and seeing oneself as romantic.

It's true that religious people tend to have fewer partners and more limitations on what practices they might include in their lovemaking. However, this takes nothing away from their desire and enjoyment of sex. Lovemaking doesn't require great variety or vast experience to be good; in fact, the opposite is true. A *Redbook* study of one hundred thousand women reveals that the earlier a woman began intercourse, and the more partners she had, the less chance she enjoyed her sex life or found satisfaction with marriage. So much for "practice makes perfect"!

On the other hand, you might be wondering what God thinks about couples who take steps to enhance their sex lives. Does He look askance at us when we strive for more pleasure, more excitement, more intensity? What did He have in mind for sexuality at the beginning of time, before Eden was corrupted?

A VIEW FROM HEAVEN

The man slept in pristine beauty, anesthetized by the sound of a crystal-clear river flowing nearby. The breeze whispered through the limbs of trees that reached to the heavens. Shrubs appeared manicured, and flowers brightly accented a carpet of grass. This portrait was animated with wildlife everywhere.

"Wake up! Look what I have for you!" came the announcement.

Slowly the man sat up, rubbed his eyes, and drank in the surrounding beauty. His eyes froze on the vision standing before him. She was a creation more beautiful than anything he'd ever seen. She stood before him nude, and neither he nor she was embarrassed.

Awestruck, he instinctively asked, "Eve?"

"Yes, Adam," she responded.

Inconspicuously, the first wedding ceremony had been performed. The Bible says God caused a great sleep to come over Adam, and while he slept, God took a rib and made a woman from it. The Creator took Eve from Adam's side, then returned His creation to him. Eve became his wife and God told them to be "fruitful and increase in number."

What observations can we make from God's account of the creation of Adam and Eve? The first thing we realize is that sex is not evil. God is the author of sex. He made men and women physically complementary, enabling them to engage in sexual intercourse. This remains God's plan. Sex is a good gift designed by the Creator Himself. No matter how sex has been abused, perverted, and deviated from God's original intent, it was designed to be a blessing to a married couple.

The male and female body were obviously made for one another. Both are desirous of sex but each gender is unique in approach and timing. Within the act of physical union lies an emotional coupling that melds two into one. This dual union defies the world's insistence that sex is a mere physical act.

Sexual intercourse was designed by God for marriage. It is

beautiful and wonderful and without disgrace—that's why Adam and Eve could stand together in the Garden naked and unashamed. It's also why God declared that man's and woman's bodies together were not just "good" but "very good." Physical bodies are important to God:

- He chose to relate to us face-to-face through Jesus' human body.
- Christ's resurrection required a body.
- We are identifiable through our bodies; there is no one who looks exactly like anyone else.
- Through the physical body, our soul (mind, will, and emotions) expresses itself and communicates.
- Bodies allow us to participate fully in God's creation.

We experience the pleasure of a sandy beach with our toes. Similarly, our bodies enable us to know the joy of holding a newborn baby, or the exquisite bliss of two bodies uniting in love. If the body is God's design and sex is God's design, sexual love cannot be evil or cursed.

"Male and female he created them." There was no shame until disobedience and a desire to be like God destroyed the harmony man, woman, and God were meant to share (Genesis 3). Only then did nakedness become a source of shame. "But in Christ, we [believers] are a new creation." The new Adam, Jesus

Christ, removed the tarnish of the first Adam's sin. Humankind has been reconciled to God and, consequently, unashamed joy and pleasure can be experienced again between a man and a woman.

THE LOVER AND THE BELOVED

Eden was not the only place sex was meant to be experienced as "unashamed." The Old Testament book titled The Song of Songs provides insight into God's plan for sex and our sexual enjoyment outside of the Garden. Two characters dominate this book, The Lover and The Beloved—the man and the woman.

The Lover declares,

> *Your graceful legs are like jewels...your neck is like an ivory tower...your hair is like royal tapestry...your navel is a rounded goblet that never lacks blended wine...your stature is like that of the palm and your breasts like clusters of wine...*

The Beloved responds,

> *His hair is wavy and black...his eyes are like doves...his legs are pillars of marble...his body is like polished ivory....*

This couple took evident pleasure in visual stimulation. But their lovemaking did not stop with the eyes:

> *His left arm is under my head and his right arm embraces me.... Let my lover come into his garden and taste his choice fruits.*

The lover and the beloved freely share each other's bodies in sexual intercourse. No sense is unimportant. There are references to sight, smell, taste, sound, and most of all, touch. They are unabashedly lost in their pleasure. The candles are clearly burning and the setting is private—no television detracts from the mood. Their bedroom was fashioned with lovemaking in mind.

Truly, God's message from His very own marriage manual is that sex is a gift meant to be enjoyed by both men and women. There are few limitations as to how the individual married couple is to make lovemaking reflect the intention of God's gift. Instead, permission is granted to the Lover and Beloved, and to us, to learn, to make mistakes, to explore, and to construct a sex life uniquely ours. Will it be unashamed? Will it be a restored Eden? Will our garden whither or blossom?

CREATING A NEW EDEN

If *Body and Soul: Understanding Your Sexual Personality* motivates you to consider the significance sex is meant to have within your marriage, that's good. If it improves your approach and communication techniques as they relate to sex, that is better. But we desire something even more magnificent for you. We want you to experience the blessing and gift of sex as God intended. We want you to have a sexual relationship that is ignited by intimacy and which meets your very personal, private, specific needs.

Even though we're hoping you'll create a new Eden in your home, our expectation is not that you will enjoy a perfect relationship. Even God doesn't expect that, for in His instructions to us about our sexuality, He includes a sexual problem. The Beloved and The Lover of Song of Songs find themselves at odds over a sexual issue. The man wants to make love but the woman is tired and uninterested. Our biblical couple is hardly distinguishable from many a modern-day scenario. Their solution is just as relevant as the problem: Both the man and the woman acknowledge and accept responsibility for their contribution to the predicament.

The man does not give his wife the silent treatment, reminding her she isn't living up to his expectations, and mumbling something about "duty." Instead, when he next sees her, he reminds her of all the things he loves and finds attractive about her.

The wife nurtures her physical desire for him by allowing herself to think lovingly and longingly about what a fine man he is, as well as how good it is to look at and touch his body.

Most importantly, the Lover and the Beloved talked—are we to do less? Do you have the skills and desire to do likewise? If you aren't sure, we hope to clarify and teach you the approach your mate will be most apt to respond to. In addition, we offer our best suggestions for improving sexual functioning by maximizing emotional and physical intimacy.

PAST PROBLEMS WITH SEX

Husbands and wives usually find their sexual relationships can be vastly enhanced by improved communication and greater emotional connection. Nevertheless, there are some couples who find themselves fitfully starting and stopping and failing to progress. For them, sex is difficult in deeper and more hurtful ways. If you are one who has experienced great difficulties with your sexual relationship(s), you may need professional help in order to learn how to experience sex as a gift of great joy and beauty.

Who are those whose sexual histories may require the intervention of a well-qualified therapist, physician, or pastor? Often they are individuals and/or couples who have experienced very broken patterns of sexuality, particularly when they were young. They may have been deprived of sexual information or overloaded with it. They may be victims of abuse—abuse frequently leaves victims feeling unworthy, unlovable, and incapable of enjoying what everyone else, they think, experiences so easily. Does this apply to you?

You are a victim of spiritual abuse if you were told...

- "God is going to punish you for that."
- "Sex is bad."
- "Talking about sex is fleshly."

You are a victim of physical abuse if you were...

- Beaten

- Slapped
- Violently mistreated

You are a victim of emotional abuse if you were told…

- "If you loved me, you'd…."
- "I never wanted you."
- "You'll never amount to anything."
- "You're a whore!"

You are a victim of sexual abuse if you experienced…

- Rape, incest, or molestation

…and/or you were told…

- "I'm only teaching you this for your own good."
- "This is our special secret."

If any of those descriptions describe you, we strongly advise you to get help from a qualified person or group. God is capable of supernatural healing and restoration even when we view our situation as hopeless.

By the way, it is important for anyone seeking help to know that healing can occur without having to recall, reveal, and confront everything and everyone from your past. Bear in mind that you can trust God to bring to mind the agenda He wants you to work on without excessive prompting from a well-meaning helper or confidant.

Besides the possibility of past abuse, there is another reason marital sexuality may be problematic. Sometimes a rupture in the marital bond is so deep that it must be addressed before anything else can be considered. Issues of infidelity and trust are foundational to a healthy marriage, and the list of things that work against a couple developing emotional and physical intimacy can be long. But that list need not defeat any couple who yearns for the idyll of the Garden—and what was meant to be.

WHERE DO WE GO FROM HERE?

Yes, sexual relationships can be challenging. But there is good news: Marital sex can be made better, and if it is already gratifying, it can be superb. Vast amounts of information and experience don't transform ordinary sex into a bit of heaven on earth. It's the simple things—like speaking to one's partner about sexual desires and preferences.

Husbands and wives who enjoy good communication about sex rate their sex life and marriage positively. The ability to talk to one another has been found to be the strongest indicator of sexual and marital satisfaction.

That's why this book can make a huge difference in your life. The DISC program, correctly used, can enhance and strengthen your own understanding of how you and your mate communicate, behave, and react. This understanding has the potential of making every aspect of your married life better, including sex.

Having in-depth knowledge and understanding means...

- Being aware of strengths, weaknesses, and blind spots
- Knowing what we want and don't want
- Understanding what we value
- Getting in touch with what we fear, as well as where we are most comfortable
- Recognizing what effectively motivates us to action.

Communication with increased depth and sensitivity intensifies feelings of affection and caring, and the end result is greater intimacy. We are all complex individuals, and marriage makes for a double set of complexities. But there is a simple equation, and you'll hear it spoken one way or another again and again before you've closed this book for the last time:

Communication leads to *greater intimacy.*

Greater intimacy leads to *wonderful sex*.

CHAPTER TWO

What Is Good Communication?

Often we work very hard at marriage, only to discover we did not establish what we were trying to accomplish. Failure to establish goals based on clear communication is a costly failure indeed. To help us avoid this problem, let's look at how to set up marriage-enriching communication goals utilizing some qualities common to all of us; we call these qualities the Four Pillars of Intimacy:

- **Common Goals**
- **Mutual Respect**
- **Tolerance**
- **Communication**

The greatest of these is *communication.* For example, we cannot establish *common goals* unless we come into agreement about what those goals are to be.

A man was moving an upright piano. Having gotten the piano stuck in a doorway, another individual came to his aid.

Both people tugged and pulled and pushed on the piano until they were exhausted.

Finally one of them declared, "We'll never get this piano out this doorway!"

To this the other person sheepishly replied, "I'm sorry; I've been trying to get it *in* the doorway."

Mutual respect is built on trust. And trust is the result of open communication proven true over a period of time. Honesty occurs when we make our words conform to reality. Integrity occurs when we consistently cause reality to conform to our words. Trust is the result of integrity, and mutual respect grows from trust.

Acceptance is the cornerstone of *tolerance*. As we invest the time required to learn more about ourselves and others, we can more readily accept others as they are, and understand why they do what they do. Acceptance and tolerance do not require that we mimic the behavior of others, condone their behavior, or even agree with it. They simply require that we be willing to understand them and accept them for who they are.

The purpose and goal of marriage and intimacy is not to change our partner but rather to celebrate him or her for being the man or woman God created—imperfections and all. In the absence of tolerance, we begin to notice all the flaws in each other. Marriages come apart when we focus on those flaws. Remember, when you were courting, how you thought those flaws were cute? Try regaining that attitude.

WHY COMMUNICATION IS ESSENTIAL

Before we start exploring our various personality types and the way they affect sexuality, we need to lay some ground rules for marital communication. Why? Because open, honest, clear communication is the foundation upon which all solid relationships are built and all intimacy is developed. No matter what our personality type, research reveals that the top three major causes for divorce are:

- Money problems
- Sexual problems
- Communication problems.

If couples begin to communicate more effectively, the problems associated with money and sex would all but evaporate. It has also been said that ninety percent of all stress management lies in improving communication.

What is communication, anyway? Volumes have been written on the subject, but here are some simple facts.

Communication,
the gateway to intimate relationships,
involves two elements:
a sender and a receiver.

In the process of communicating, the sender encodes information and transmits it to the receiver. Normally this is done verbally. The receiver then decodes the information, processes it mentally, and responds to the sender with something called feedback. Feedback is the receiver's reaction to what the sender has said or done.

Feedback comes in two basic forms—verbal and nonverbal (popularly called "body language"). The nonverbal aspect of communication is very important:

- Fifty-five percent of our ability to communicate is nonverbal
- Thirty-eight percent is our tone of voice—not what we say, but how we say it
- Seven percent of our total communications behavior involves the actual words that we use, and their content.

Only seven percent! There are several factors that also affect communication. Here are a few...

Age

Values

Vocabulary

Culture

Knowledge

Gender

Personality style

Emotions

Language

Noise (internal and external)

Considering all the distractions that exist, it isn't surprising that many couples do not talk as much as they should. More amazing is how rarely they talk about sex, and this certainly isn't because the subject is socially taboo. Sex is everywhere—television, movies, books, magazines, computer on-line services, even sermons at church. Nonetheless, many couples remain inhibited when it comes to talking about their personal sex lives.

This is worth repeating: One of the primary ways to improve your sex life is to talk about it, to be open and honest, and to listen to the heart and soul of your partner. However, communication can be difficult.

When it comes to the human personality and the behavioral style emanating from your personality, eighty-four percent of us are listeners while the other sixteen percent are tellers. (You will read more about personality styles in the next chapter.)

That sixteen percent is badly in need of becoming better listeners, and the rest are desperately in need of becoming more talkative. But still we aren't in touch the way we should be. Why don't we communicate? The answer: vulnerability.

"If I let you into my life, really let you know who I am, what I feel, what I want and what I don't want, I might not be good enough for you. You might reject me. My security with you could be threatened. You might criticize me, or you might even take advantage of the knowledge I share with you and get the upper hand."

A DECISION TO COMMUNICATE

Jim was well acquainted with those feelings. Connie, his wife of twenty-five years, was a wonderful woman who listened, cared, and prayed. Jim was a "teller," not a "listener," but he told selectively only what would make him look good. His greatest fear in life was the fear of being rejected. He reasoned that if he told his wife some of the deep secrets of his life, she might use that in the future to take advantage of him. That's the way he felt early in his marriage, and like most of us, he had a secret.

Before meeting Connie, and before he met the Lord, Jim had developed a taste for X-rated movies. He was tremendously aroused by them, so he masturbated while he watched. After he and Connie were married, he realized how wrong X-rated movies were and he stopped watching them, but the temptation remained. From time to time, when he was away from home on business, Jim purchased a pay-per-view soft-porn movie in his hotel room and allowed it to seduce him.

There were occasions at home, too, when a magazine, film, or book led him astray. It didn't happen every week, and not even every month, but when it did happen, it affected the couple's lovemaking.

The two had just attended a seminar about communication and sharing with spouses, led by Howard Hendricks and J. Allan Petersen. Jim decided to risk everything after the seminar. He asked Connie to take a drive with him. As they drove, he searched for courage. Finally, he broke the silence.

"Connie," he started, "I really do love you, but I'm about to tell you something I've been keeping a secret for a long time. After I tell you, you may want to leave me. If you do, I'll understand."

Horror shadowed Connie's face, and Jim wasn't sure if she was ready for the confession of his life. Of course Connie was expecting the worst, thinking she had been the most naive person in the world in not recognizing her husband's illicit affair with another woman.

"All right, here goes!" Jim burst out. His hands clenched into white-knuckled fists. The sound of his own words frightened him. "I've had this problem with fantasizing and masturbation for several years."

Connie caught her breath, and involuntarily laughed.

"It's not funny," Jim said, staring at her.

"No, Jim, it's not, but I'm so relieved. I thought you were going to tell me you were having an affair or something like that."

"Aren't you upset?" He studied her face, unsure how to read her thoughts.

"Jim, I recognize that this is a serious problem." Connie put her hand gently on her husband's arm. "And I know how hard it was for you to tell me. I just want you to answer one question…"

"What's that?" Jim braced himself.

"What can I do to help? I mean, besides praying."

Weak with gratitude, Jim looked out the window. He hesitated for a minute or two, collecting his thoughts. "When I'm traveling, I think it would help if I called you when I'm tempted... Maybe we could talk about it or pray together."

Connie nodded. "Jim, I'd like to ask another question. Is our sex life satisfying you? Are you looking for something you don't have with me? If so, let's talk about that..."

And so the dialogue went.

Before the afternoon was over, Jim and Connie prayed together, developed a strategy to overcome temptation, renewed a vow to be vulnerable through communication, and felt closer to each other than at any moment since the day they were married.

Was Jim ever tempted again? Yes. Did he ever succumb to the temptation again? Not often. He had taken off his mask and enlarged the communication arena to include Connie's prayerful supportive love, and the power of God. Their marriage was stronger than ever.

THREE KEY FACTS ABOUT COMMUNICATION

Here are the facts you need to remember when considering communication.

- Communication is risky business because through it we become very vulnerable.

- Communication is worth the risk because without self-disclosure, intimacy is impossible to attain.
- Your spouse can handle a lot more truth than you think.

The difficult art of communication is a means of healing and growth. As Willard Harley, Jr., points out, conversation allows you to:

1. Communicate needs to each other
2. Learn how to meet each other's needs.[1]

Charley Shedd observes that marriage is a relationship where two can say, "I want to know you. I want you to know me. Let us begin learning who we are and sharing who we are, no reservations."[2]

PAINTING WORD PICTURES

Assuming we agree to improve our communication skills, where do we start? One valuable technique is the use of word pictures. Women use this method of expression far more often than men, and males would do well to become more adept at utilizing this valuable communication tool.

Word pictures allow others to literally "see" what we are saying. Furthermore, they unlock the door to the emotions behind the words. These pictures allow us to listen to others with empathy, to get in touch with the feelings that are being expressed, and to understand the words we hear.

This is not a new idea. Many of the world's great communicators have used word pictures to get their point across. The greatest of these was Jesus Christ. He spoke in parables and used many metaphors to help people understand what He was saying. His vivid illustrations—such as stories about the Good Samaritan and the Prodigal Son—are recalled by churched and unchurched people alike.

We all use word pictures every day, often without realizing it. When spouses use them when speaking, they begin to bridge the gap of understanding between the two sexes. As you'll discover in Chapter Eight, women have a need to verbalize their emotions and feelings. Men have a need to put emotions into a logical frame of reference. The use of word pictures enables both male and female needs to be met. Here are some hints for effectively creating and using word pictures.

- **Make sure you paint a word picture that has a specific purpose.** Use it to praise, to clarify a point, to offer corrective feedback, or to build intimacy. Word pictures can be used very effectively for all of these.

- **Center your picture around something relative to the interests of the other person.** He or she will be able to grasp the concept or feeling you are trying to convey because of familiarity with the context in which it is being presented.

- **Timing is everything.** Make sure your word pictures, and your purpose for using them, are well timed.

Where do we get our word pictures? The sources are practically endless, but we can begin to learn to look at life with this purpose in mind. Maybe you've been to Disneyland or Disney World recently. If so, you might paint a word picture something like this:

"I don't understand it, Marie. You seemed as eager as I was to make love. So what happened?" John looked genuinely perplexed. He leaned against the headboard and glanced over at his wife of six months.

Marie was reaching for a tissue to wipe away her tears. "I don't know, John. I love you, and I want to make love. But it seems that as soon as we walk into the bedroom, everything moves so fast, and I feel overwhelmed."

"I ask you what you want..." John replied, somewhat defensively.

Marie nodded. "I know you do, but it seems to me that once your motor is roaring, you take off on something that feels like Mr. Toad's Wild Ride. I'm too busy hanging on for dear life to enjoy the sights along the way, or to make suggestions about stopping or changing course."

You may be thinking, *I wouldn't describe sex like that if someone held a gun to my head!* Please remember, the picture is not for you, it's for your spouse. This picture communicates the feelings and emotions that accompanied the situation. This is what he or she needs to hear.

Good sources of word pictures are all around us: material objects, memories, comparisons to other people, or whatever comes to mind. With a little thought, creativity, and practice, you can become quite good at this. (It will be especially challenging to "D's" and "C's," but more about that later!)

TRUST BUILDERS

As we begin to understand each other and to communicate a bit better, trust begins to grow. Trust, honesty, self-esteem, and understanding are important to both men and women. For intimacy to grow in our relationships, we must move into a place of open and honest communication. There is a model for building this type of communication in relationships, known as the Johari Window. The Johari Window looks like this (see chart 2.1):

THE ARENA I know and You know A place of TRUST	**BLIND SPOTS** You know and I don't
MASK I know and You don't	**POTENTIAL** We both don't know

Luft, Joseph. Of Human Interaction, Palo Alto, Calif.: Mayfield Publishing Co., 1969

The Arena—The place of trust. This is where each person knows about the other. Masks are discarded and blind spots are shared. Our goal in the Arena is to increase trust to encompass the entire window.

Blind Spots—These are things the other person does of which he or she is unaware. We all have blind spots. They are personality aspects that are hidden from us.

The Mask—There are things a person knows about but does not wish to share with anyone else. These are hidden by a mask. This is where the secrets that destroy intimacy and relationship lurk. Secrets can make a relationship sick.

Potential—This is the least predictable. It is also a place of the future and the unknown. Most stresses in life are caused by a lack of information.

If we truly desire intimacy in a relationship, our goal is to move into the Arena as quickly as possible and to make it expand, through open and honest communication based on trust. As we look at each of the four blocks, our desire is to replace what is there with "I know and You know."

We want to open up and share things about ourselves with our partner, intentionally removing masks.

We want to approach blind spots, taking the risk to do so in a very nonthreatening and noncritical way to prevent defensiveness.

We want to explore unknowns together, without fear and with a sense of mutual discovery.

To accomplish this kind of open and honest communication, we need to understand who our partner really is, and learn to "speak his or her language."

THE FINE ART OF LISTENING

Besides learning to communicate with word pictures, and to establish open dialogue, we all need to listen with greater sensitivity. In fact, we can greatly improve our listening skills by learning to C-A-R-E—Connect, Attend, Reflect, and Empathize.

• ***CONNECT with your partner nonverbally.*** The goal is to gain rapport, to mirror him or her in the interaction. Take time to observe your spouse's body language and do everything you can to complement it. If he or she is using eye contact, or leaning forward, you may want to do the same. If he or she is employing touch, you may want to match that, depending on your husband or wife's personality style. Pace yourself and your presentation to his or her pace. If your spouse is relaxed, you need to relax. If he or she is sitting up straight, you need to do the same, and so on. Find a way to connect yourself to your partner and what he or she is saying.

• ***Learn to ATTEND (pay heed to) your partner.*** The value of paying attention lies in the feelings of self-esteem it gives to the person toward whom we are directing our attention. It has been a tradition in the military for centuries that when someone of great importance enters the area, everyone comes to "attention." Paying attention to people is a good way to demonstrate how much we respect and value them.

Often the entire purpose of our marital interaction is to secure time and attention from one another. Let's not short-change our spouse in this regard. There are four things that are communicated when we pay attention: Honor, Respect, Commitment, and Meaningful Communication.

• ***REFLECT—be quiet and still.*** Have you ever seen your reflection in a pond that was still as glass? What happened to your image when something disturbed the surface of the water? Sometimes we are so busy doing that we lose sight of *why* we are doing something. Reflection is taking time to plan, review, process, and let people know we've really heard what they've said.

• ***EMPATHIZE to get in touch with the other's feelings.*** We don't necessarily need to agree with someone to show him empathy. We simply need to share the emotions he is expressing and understand how and why he feels that way.

SILENCE IS GOLDEN—SOMETIMES

In Scripture, we read that there is a "time to be silent and a time to speak." When we stop talking, we fall silent, and that silence can be peaceful. It can stimulate further communication. Or it can be threatening, even terrifying. There are many types of silence:

- ***The pregnant pause.*** This is a strategic break in the communication designed to allow ideas to gestate, be birthed and adopted, or rejected.

- ***Unspoken rapport.*** When two people are truly in sync with each other, as Scripture says, "being of one flesh," they often communicate in silence, and the rapport can be deafening.

- ***No comment necessary.*** Some silence is necessary to maintain the relationship. This occurs when we realize it is better to say nothing.

- ***A loss for words.*** Silence can be embarrassing or uncomfortable because we don't know what to say.

- ***An angry tactic.*** Like sex and affection, silence can be a weapon. Have you ever given or received the dreaded "silent treatment"? The degree to which this silence affects us depends largely on our personality style. It can often be very painful.

- ***Stubborn avoidance.*** Sometimes silence is the result of problem evasion: "I don't want to talk about it." This isn't good because it keeps masks on, perpetuates blind spots, and moves us away from the arena of trust. One thing is certain—even in silence, communication is taking place.

WORDS ARE IMPORTANT

Once the silence is broken, the words we use are very important. Our words can destroy or build up. Richard, a teenager perpetually in trouble with authority figures, was the clown of the church youth group. He also was desperately lonely. One day in Duane's office he confessed, "All I can remember Dad saying to me is how stupid I am and how much trouble I am to him and Mom."

Were these words true? Not from what Duane observed, but words are powerful. The writer of Proverbs declared, "The tongue has the power of life and death" (Proverbs 18:21, NIV).

After years of destructive words, couples sometimes give up and their marriage ends. A simple sentence like, "You're a terrible housekeeper," or "You're a rotten lover; I don't know why I married you," can devastate a partner. Words can rip the heart out of the soul of a marriage.

But words can also be used to heal, build up, and bring life into a relationship. "An anxious heart weighs a man down, but a kind word cheers him up" (Proverbs 12:25, NIV).

The subject of speech is so important that the Book of James speaks volumes in one poignant verse, "The tongue also is a fire, a world of evil among the parts of the body. It corrupts the whole person" (James 3:6, NIV). The tongue is like the rudder that steers a large cruise ship. It determines the direction of the ship. Similarly, the direction of a relationship between husband and wife can be steered by words.

So important is our speech that the gospel of Matthew tells us, "For by your words you will be acquitted and by your words you will be condemned" (Matthew 12:37, NIV). Sometimes our language exposes us. The way we speak of our spouse reveals our self-centeredness or our yieldedness to God. It reveals the condition of our soul.

One of the leading causes for marital difficulty is our unwillingness to use positive language and compliments that build up, using instead negative words which tear down.

How long has it been since you've said...

- "I love you."
- "Have I told you how wonderful you are lately? Well, you are!"
- "You really turn me on!"
- "I like your body."
- "I can't imagine my sexual life being more wonderful than you're making it."
- "You're like a breath of fresh air to my life."
- "Thank you! You're terrific!"

How would you feel if those words were spoken to you? They make your partner feel the same way. Every time positive, kind words are spoken, our partners are encouraged.

TAKE TIME TO TALK

Within marriages, the great common denominator of all people is time. God has given you, and everyone else in existence, only 1,440 minutes in every day. No more, and no less. Your choice is to invest this precious resource in the hope of reaping a generous return, or to spend it foolishly and watch it slip away, never to be recaptured.

The time we invest talking and listening with our spouse is time well spent. The more time we devote to expanding the Arena of Trust, the greater our intimacy dividends will be. The greater the depth of understanding we can achieve with one another, the closer we will come to enjoying the intended benefits of God's sexual plan for us.

It was a quiet Saturday afternoon, and author Duane was watching the Colorado Buffaloes playing football on TV. His wife, Marty, had just returned from shopping. She marched into the living room and announced, "I just hate shopping at Tammy's store. I know she's a Christian and goes to our church but I'm not going back."

It was a close game and Colorado was moving down the field, ready to score the winning touchdown with only two minutes left in the game. Duane was intently watching each play.

"Hi, Babes!" he said, acknowledging her presence and then quickly returning his attention to the game.

"Aren't you going to answer me?" she asked, a little upset by his lack of response.

Before he could say a word, she rambled on, "Every time I go there, she puts Vern down."

He probably deserves it, Duane thought, *especially if I don't see this winning touchdown.*

"She never stops!" Marty was on a roll! "He's not a good provider. 'Lazy' she calls him. He doesn't meet her needs, smells bad because he doesn't bathe regularly..."

Duane could see she wasn't going to let up. With one eye on the game, he turned his head and asked, "Have you talked to her about it?" *Please, Lord, don't let me miss this score; then I'll talk.*

"Yes, but it doesn't do any good. She doesn't stop!"

Forget the game. We're going to communicate, whether I think it's the right time or not. Duane clicked off the TV. He realized his desire to stay current with his favorite college football team was greatly outweighed in importance by his wife's need for him to spend some time talking with her. His attentiveness, even if somewhat reluctantly rendered, expanded the Arena of Trust in their marriage.

We often hear people say, "I just don't have any time!" A more accurate statement perhaps would be, "I don't prioritize my time well." For example, did you know...

- The average adult American watches 37.8 hours of television per week.[3]
- The average American father spends about two and a half minutes per day with his children.[4]
- Sixty-nine percent of our children will spend at least six months of their life in a single-parent home before reaching the age of twelve.[5]

An old adage reminds us that no person on his death bed has ever said, "I should have spent more time at the office!"

Open and honest communication builds trust and intimacy into our marriage relationships. To accomplish this level of interaction, however, we have a lot to learn. How well do we really know each other? Greater self-knowledge can transform the quality of our conversations. And an understanding of our spouse's personality can change the way we speak, listen, and respond. Read on to discover surprising insights about yourself, and about the one you love.

OPPORTUNITIES FOR GROWTH

Respond to the following questions with your spouse.

1. In what five ways do I communicate with you well?

2. What two things can I do to communicate with you more effectively?

3. In what ways do you feel that I listen to you with CARE?

4. How can I improve my CARE skills in listening?

5. List three ways in which better communication would improve our relationship, intimacy, or sexuality.

CHAPTER 2 Endnotes

1. Willard F. Harley, Jr., *His Needs, Her Needs* (Grand Rapids, Michigan: Fleming H. Revell, 1986), p. 62.

2. Charlie and Martha Shedd, *Celebration In the Bedroom* (Dallas, Texas: Word Books, 1979), p. 48.

3. From a pamphlet, "Did Television Cause the Changes…?" by David Barton (Aledo, Texas: Wallbuilder Press, 1989).

4. Quote taken from a *Focus on the Family* radio broadcast in 1991; the program was hosted by Dr. James Dobson.

5. Quote taken from a *Focus on the Family* radio broadcast in 1991; the program was hosted by Dr. James Dobson.

CHAPTER THREE

Discovering Your Personality Type

Don doesn't like to be told what to do but he doesn't mind ordering everyone else around. Some people think he is a control freak, but Don sees it differently. Being on top of everything eliminates surprises and allows him to accomplish whatever needs to be done. It also ensures that no one is going to get one-up on him. While Don is sometimes hard to be around, he can usually be depended on in a crisis to come through with a creative and visionary solution. Have you ever wondered what makes a person like Don tick? If you are like Don yourself, or are married to a Don, are you interested in knowing how his personality style handles relationships, sex, and intimacy?

Few have a problem being around Isabella. She's friendly—loves to talk and seems to really like most people. She isn't always on time, but once she arrives, you'll have her full attention. And if she forgets her lunch date with you, she'll show up at your door with flowers and an "I'm So Sorry" greeting card. Ever wonder what someone like Isabella is really like? Liking people as much as she does, do you think she could ever really be satisfied within a marriage? Is it possible you are a male "Isabella"? What would happen if Isabella married Don? Would you want them in your neighborhood?

The neighborhood might be considerably quieter if it were filled with people like Steve. Steve is one of those "nice" guys who is quiet and steady and sticks to his business. He seems to love his family very much and spends most weekends puttering around the house. Is Steve just a good guy or is he actually basically dull? Would he take any risks in lovemaking if he doesn't seem to take many in other areas of his life? If you were married to a Steve, or a female version of Steve, what approach would transform him or her into a great lover? Do you know the crucial ingredient necessary to motivate Steve's full expression in sexuality?

Cindy writes poetry. She has great depth and is a loyal spouse and worker. She functions best when she is told clearly and succinctly what you expect of her. If her life becomes hectic and unorganized, Cindy is prone to getting discouraged. She often feels responsible for things that aren't her responsibility, and can put tremendous pressure on herself. Are you Cindy? Are you married to someone like her?

What is it that makes Don, Isabella, Steve, and Cindy think, act, and make choices so consistently? More importantly, what makes you and your spouse think, act, and make the choices that you do?

PERSONALITY BY DIVINE PLAN

Our personalities were formed in the mind of God before we were born, even before we were conceived in the womb. We read in Psalm 139: 13-16 (NIV):

> For you created my inmost being; you knit me together in my mother's womb. I praise you because I am fearfully and wonderfully made; your works are wonderful, I know that full well. My frame was not hidden from you when I was made in the secret place. When I was woven together in the depths of the earth, your eyes saw my unformed body. All the days ordained for me were written in your book before one of them came to be.

NATURE OR NURTURE?

How did you get to be who you are? How about your spouse? How much of a role did heredity play in shaping you? What about environment? Were you born this way or did you become this way? For years there has been an ongoing debate in the psychological community about the influence of

NATURE

(Heredity)

versus

NURTURE

(Environment, Role Models, etc.)

Some experts believe that everything springs from nature. Others subscribe to the nurture theory. The truth probably contains a little bit of each theory, coupled with a generous helping of God's design, making you who He meant you to be in the first place.

From the time you were born, you have been attempting to satisfy your needs. In the beginning you cried, screamed, cooed, grunted, or simply reached for what you wanted. As you got older, you began to develop a more sophisticated and complex set of behaviors designed to obtain what you needed. While this process was taking place, your resident personality was emerging.

"YOU HAVEN'T CHANGED A BIT"

This personality was further defined and shaped by various external influences such as role models, your environment, relationships with others, and a myriad of learning experiences. By the time you were three and a half to five years of age, some fairly consistent patterns or styles of behavior could be readily observed.

Have you ever had the experience of listening to older family members reminisce about you or your siblings?

> *"Remember how little Bobby was always showing off? He just had to be the center of attention—all the time."*

> *"It was so funny to watch Janie play with her doll house. All the furniture had to be arranged just so. She was really bossy, even with her dolls."*

"Did I ever tell you about the time Timmy took his father's radio apart just to see how it worked? I'll be darned if he didn't put it back together all by himself!"

"Remember how Betty Ann and Connie were just the best of friends? Even now, they're closer than twin sisters."

And how about those dreaded report card comments...

"Roger doesn't play well with others; he seems to prefer to be by himself."

"Sally needs to be more organized; she loses things and does not complete her work on time. She is just not working up to her potential."

"Andrea needs to spend less time socializing and concentrate more on her studies."

"Robert does not participate well in class. He seems to be painfully shy."

THREE BASIC ENVIRONMENTS

Do any of the above statements sound familiar? They are all observations based on the personality and behavioral style of children. Most likely, though, you still exhibit some of those patterns today, at least to a degree.

Your personality style helps determine how you behave in efforts to satisfy your needs. This, however, is only the tip of the iceberg. Everything you...

Hear...

See...

Say...

Fear...

Perceive...

Think...

Act upon...

is influenced by your personality and dictates your behavioral style.

How intense is your personality style? Its intensity will dictate the way you behave to satisfy your needs. The environment you are in, and your perception of that environment, will also influence how you behave.

Our personality styles are always evolving. Therefore, it's dangerous to "pigeon hole" people. As we develop a profile for you, we hope to provide you with insights. We want you to have a snapshot of your personality style *as it is today*.

Five years from now, you may have changed a great deal. But no matter what the season of your life, everyone lives in one of three basic environments most of the time. These three are the...

Home Environment

Work Environment

Social Environment

OUR THREE SELVES

Within these three environments, you will manifest three variations of your personality style, which are:

The Mask, or Public Self: This is the personality style that you project to others.

The Core, or Private Self: This is the personality style that has become your instinctive response to pressure or stress.

The Mirror, or Perceived Self: This is the personality style which results from your sense of self-image.[1]

It is possible for you to exhibit three different personality variations of your basic personality style in any environment. (No, you are not suffering from Multiple Personality Disorder—this is normal, so don't worry!)

Not only do we live and function in these three basic environments, but we also have a need to control, or at least exert an influence over, each environment in which we find ourselves. Put another way, we attempt to redesign our environment to make it more comfortable. And we try to mold relationships to meet the demands of our personality, rather than adjusting our personality to meet the demands of the relationship.

REACTING TO FEAR

Each of us has a basic fear that colors our perception of the environment in which we find ourselves. That fear, coupled with our need to control our environment (so we will feel comfortable in it), motivates us to some type of action or inaction. Our basic fear stems from our personality. As a result of this basic fear and the need to overcome it, we perceive things in a particular way and we will be motivated to avoid unpleasant experiences.

Let's take a look at how four basic fears act out. Once you've studied these fears, you'll see how they correlate with the four personality types that follow.

If your basic fear is being taken advantage of you may perceive an environment as antagonistic or hostile. To change or control the environment to avoid this fear, you will adjust your behavior accordingly. You would become dominant, direct, active, assertive, or even aggressive in your attempts to gain and maintain control. "The best defense is a good offense," or "A moving target is harder to hit," or "Trust me," may be some of your favorite mottoes. In addition, you may be a bit suspicious of those who ask a lot of questions, move slowly, or get bogged down in details.

If your basic fear is loss of social approval your perception of the environment will usually be favorable. As a result, you will work very hard to keep it favorable, and to gain acceptance from others. In order to avoid loss of social approval, you will be friendly, outgoing, talkative, demonstrative, diplomatic, and people-pleasing. You will also try to influence others to your point of view.

If your basic fear is loss of security, you may still perceive your environments as favorable. But your approach to avoiding this fear may be cautious, slow-paced, methodical, relational, friendly, trusting, or submitting. You want to maintain the status-quo since you are secure with the way things are now. As long as you feel secure, you see little reason to "rock the boat" by changing things.

If your basic fear is criticism or change in circumstances, you may see the environment as unfavorable. Your response in avoiding this fear may be much more tentative, cautious, analytical, detail-oriented, structured, compliant, systematic, organized, and exact. You may be slow to change or work hard to avoid being criticized. You may want things to be absolutely correct according to your own set of standards. You would want to know all the details about every aspect of a situation before making a decision. Furthermore, you will avoid confrontation at almost any cost.

Just as there are four basic fears that motivate us, there are four primary personality styles. Of course there are myriad combinations, and there are variations of our personalities in different environments. You may notice that although you strongly reflect one of these styles at work, you are quite different at home. But the basic patterns remain.

THE DOMINANT DIRECTOR

The first personality style we want to take a closer look at is the **Dominant Director**, or **"D."** These men and women tend to be task-oriented and display affection based on what you do for them. If you do what they say, they like you. If you make a deal with them and break your deal, you will cease to exist in their world. They'll just draw an "X" through your name and you're history!

This dominant personality style makes up approximately three percent of the population. Any more than that and we'd be at war all the time!

On the positive side, the world needs Dominant Directors. They tend to be visionaries, leading us in the right direction. They are decisive and are willing to take risks to keep relationships together. Inventive and creative, they initiate action in their relationships and move when others lag behind. During a crisis, they normally stay focused and accomplish what needs to be done.

THE INFLUENCER

The second personality style is the **Influencer**, or **"I."** They like to talk, and they try to make themselves easy to love. They tend to be outgoing, optimistic, and friendly. In fact, when you get a couple of these people together, you either have the "mutual admiration society" or a party, because they talk and they talk and they talk. They want to have fun, and they enjoy talking to you. Sometimes, while they're talking to you they'll reach out and touch you. After all, even if you just met them, you're hitting it off, right?

Influencers make up approximately eleven percent of the population, and they are very communicative. If there were any more than that, buy all the telephone stock you can and you'd make money. These are the communicators with a people-oriented focus. They are encouragers and will lift your spirits in times of trouble. They have a contagious enthusiasm, a good sense of humor, and bring hope into situations that may appear hopeless.

THE STEADY RELATOR

The third style, which represents about sixty-nine percent of the population, we'll call the **Steady Relator,** or **"S."** These people tend to be easygoing, steady, stable, family-oriented, relational, compassionate, and they don't like any confrontation. However, don't for a moment think they are pushovers. They have very definite ideas about how things ought to be and once they have made up their mind, they don't move. God's wisdom is evident in the fact that so many people are this style. These people are the glue that holds the fabric of society together. They are team players and, more often than not, especially in a relationship, will be the peace-makers and nurturers. Building intimacy comes naturally to the Steady Relator. They have the ability to stay on course and offer comfort to those who are hurting.

THE CONSCIENTIOUS THINKER

The fourth personality style is the **Conscientious Thinker**, or "**C.**" They tend to be compliant, correct, conscientious, perfectionist, precise, and exact. They like to track the progress of things. They are task-oriented but enjoy doing things systematically. Tasks that have a clearly defined beginning, middle, and end appeal to them. These people enjoy creating systems and making lists. Talking is not something they do a lot, but they never forget things. This style makes up about seventeen percent of the population. Intimacy for the Conscientious Thinker may revolve around analyzing and arriving at the proper solutions, or sharing ideas. They have a depth of insight that allows them to see what others do not. They can get to the heart of a matter by going beyond the superficial.

DO YOU RECOGNIZE ANYONE?

I'm sure that as you read through the characteristics of the four personality styles, you picked up on some things that sounded as if they were written about you. You undoubtedly recognized some things about your spouse, as well. In the following chapters, we will go into much greater detail about the four primary styles. We will begin this process by completing a simple personality assessment. Through this instrument, you will discover that you may have a combination of more than one of these styles resident within you.

Actually, each of us has *all four styles* within us. While we may have one style, or a combination of styles, that is dominant, we have the ability to bring up elements of all four when we need them to meet the demands of a particular situation or environment. This ability to modify our own style and successfully blend it with the style of another person is truly a gift from God.

When used properly, an awareness of personality types can literally change a relationship from "Hell on Earth" to "Almost Heaven." We know this to be true because we have personally seen it happen for tens of thousands of people. All you need is an open mind, a willingness to change the way you have done things in the past, and the Grace of God. Please complete the Style Overview Sampler™ Personality Assessment[2] before moving on to the next chapters.

DIRECTIONS FOR COMPLETING THE STYLE OVERVIEW SAMPLER™

1. During the course of our day, most of us move between and operate in three basic environments: Home, Work, and Social. For the purposes of this book, please respond only in the

"Home" environment. For example, as you respond to each statement, consider, "At home with my spouse, I am..."

2. On the following page (chart 3.1), read across the columns from left to right. In descending order, rank the selections in each of the fifteen categories that best describe you in your chosen environmental focus. Use a 4 for the statement that is most like you, working down to a 1 to indicate the statement that is least like you.

3. Once you have made all of your selections, add your scores vertically and total them in the boxes below marked "D," "I," "S," and "C." Now follow the directions (See Chart 3.2 on page 68) in the box marked "Instructions for Graphing Your Results..."

STYLE OVERVIEW SAMPLER								
My sexual Personality is mostly...	Commanding Direct		Outgoing Expressive		Easygoing Informal		No-Nonsense Precise	
I prefer an environment where I am surrounded by...	Trophies Awards Charts		Clutter Pictures My "Stuff"		Keepsakes Mementos Comfort		Order Functionality Organization	
My personal style tends to be...	Results Oriented		People Oriented		Process/Team Oriented		Detail Oriented	
My manner of responding to others is...	Impatient Restless		Friendly Obliging		Steady Reserved		Cool Detached	
When listening to others I...	Often become impatient		Find my attention drifting		Am willing to listen carefully		Am selective and focus on facts	
I enjoy talking to others...	About my achievements		About myself and other people		About my family and friends		About things, systems or organizations	
In relationships I tend to...	Command others		Empathize with others		Accept others		Assess others	
When making decisions I lean toward...	Being quick or impulsive		Doing what's popular *or* my emotional response		Becoming slow, cautious, and/or studied		Staying objective and/or fact-based	
In terms of my time usage, I find that...	I'm always pressed for time		I tend to socialize at the expense of time		I respect time but I'm not easily pushed		I value and manage my time well	
The pace at which I live is...	Fast		Enthusiastic		Steady		Controlled	
My normal tone of voice is...	Emotional and direct		Emotional and animated		Unemotional and low-keyed		Unemotional and reserved	
My gestures seem to most often be...	Impatient		Open		Measured		Closed	
My prefered mode of dress is...	Formal		Stylish		Conforming		Conservative	
My overall manner could be described as...	Domineering or controlling		Friendly or outgoing		Accepting or open		Evaluating or reserved	
My conversation centers around...	Getting to the "bottom line"		People and items relating to them		"How to's" and/or relationships		Facts, information, and data	
TOTALS	**D**		**I**		**S**		**C**	

CHART 3.1

Instructions for Graphing Your Results...

1. Check the accuracy of the totals for each of the D,I,S, and C columns. All four columns, when totaled together, should equal 150.
2. Now, plot the number from each column on the adjacent graph. Example: If you have scored 39 in the D column, place a dot on the number 39 under the D.
3. Draw lines to connect your D,I,S, and C dots, moving from the D to the I, S, and C.
4. Circle the highest point on your graph.

D	I	S	C
60	60	60	60
57	57	57	57
54	54	54	54
51	51	51	51
48	48	48	48
45	45	45	45
42	42	42	42
39	39	39	39
36	36	36	36
33	33	33	33
30	30	30	30
27	27	27	27
24	24	24	24
21	21	21	21
18	18	18	18
15	15	15	15

CHART 3.2

Following the instructions in Chart 3.2 for completing the profile on page 67, we would like to suggest that Chart 3.3 as shown below is an example of how a completed row should look.

EXAMPLE...

My sexual Personality is mostly...	Commanding Direct	4	Outgoing Expressive	2	Easygoing Informal	3	No-Nonsense Precise	1
I prefer an environment where I am surrounded by...	Trophies Awards Charts	3	Clutter Pictures My "Stuff"	4	Keepsakes Mementos Comfort	1	Order Functionality Organization	2
My personal style tends to be...	Results Oriented	2	People Oriented	4	Process/Team Oriented	3	Detail Oriented	1

CHART 3.2

Have you had an interesting journey through the characteristics, tendencies, strengths, and weaknesses of all four personality styles? We hope you've had a few chuckles and gained some good insights along the way. There are many more fascinating discoveries ahead for you.

It has been said many times that knowledge is power. We believe that the true power of knowledge lies in the options it provides us. Each of us has made a choice—a decision to love someone else. By learning more about them and ourselves, we can now choose to relate to them in a way that will enhance our intimacy rather than detract from it. Remember...

- You are a combination of all four styles, so different parts of what we have discussed will apply to you.
- You can be a different instinctive style in response to the demands of your various environments. Try to focus on home, relationship, and intimacy.
- Our personalities are always evolving. The way you are today may not be the way you will always be. There is great hope in knowing that God equipped us with the capacity to change when necessary—all we need is the willingness to do so.

CHAPTER 3 Endnotes

1. References to the *Mask* or Public Self, the *Core* or Private Self, and the *Mirror* or Perceived Self are taken from the Personality System Profile, copyright ©The Institute for Motivational Living, Inc. All rights reserved.

2. The Style Overview Sampler™ is an abbreviated version of The Personality System Profile™, and was adapted specifically for publication in this volume. Copyright ©The Institute for Motivational Living, Inc. All rights reserved.

CHAPTER FOUR

The Dominant Director

Donna heard the car enter the driveway and rushed to pick up the mess Jamie had left on the dining room table. "Just once," she muttered to herself, "I'd like everything to be perfect when Don walks into this house." She paused and chuckled, "Fat chance that will happen! Trust him to see something I've overlooked."

"Hi, Hon!" Don called as he burst through the door, replacing a bag of cat litter on the shelf while storing his keys in just the right spot on the key rack. Swinging into the kitchen, he asked, "Where's Jamie? I thought this was his homework time."

Donna tried to look composed. She hadn't seen their son for the last hour and she had been enjoying the peace and quiet. Jamie hated coming home from school only to have to sit down and do homework. She agreed with him.

Don, however, was a firm believer that "business" was first, play second, even for eight-year-olds. Before she had time to answer, Don announced they would need to have a family meeting where Jamie's infraction would be discussed.

Don really was a nice guy. He had lots of enthusiasm and energy, and like others of his "D" temperament, he had more things to do than time to do them. He was a good organizer who excelled at his management job, and he was often frustrated by the fact that his family was less manageable than his subordinates. He didn't have a lot of patience with excuses and, truthfully, Donna and Jamie were a little frightened of his overbearing manner when they didn't perform up to his expectations.

Don's tendency to dominate and control carried over to the bedroom. Two nights earlier, for example, sex had again been a disappointment to them both. When Don was through, Donna had rolled over and faced the wall. Out of her tightly closed eyes, one tear had fought its way out and over the bridge of her nose, silently disappearing into the pillowcase. Donna wished she could disappear, too.

It seemed to her that their sex life had always been a one-way street. She sincerely wanted to respond and in the past she had, but lately the very prospect of lovemaking filled her with anxiety. She wondered if she would ever again experience an orgasm.

Don was upset, too, and his response was none too subtle. He had begun to bring home books and articles on the subject, and had tried to suggest various self-help routines. Instead of helping, each article and book had reinforced Donna's guilt and made her feel more inept.

Last night had been the worst experience yet. Don had mumbled something about "making love to a dead fish" before storming off to the bathroom. When he returned, he announced in his most no-nonsense voice, "Donna, I won't put up with this. There is no reason for you not to have an orgasm. I'm making you an appointment with a therapist. Maybe he or she can help you get your act together."

UNDERSTANDING THE DOMINANT DIRECTOR

Let's take a look at some of the general tendencies of the High "D," or Dominant Director, personality style. This style is characterized by active, positive movement in what is perceived to be an antagonistic environment.

In the last chapter we discussed how each person's greatest fear results in a unique environmental viewpoint. The greatest fear of the Dominant Director is being taken advantage of. For this reason, these individuals tend to view any environment they are in as antagonistic. Since a good offense is the best defense, they try to control their environment by being forceful, positive, and active.

Dominant Directors are extroverted, active doers who tend to be optimistic but are not overly relational or instinctively intimate.

To help you recognize the "D," here is a quick reference list of their most common characteristics:

1. They have a high ego strength, seek authority, and enjoy initiating action.
2. They tend to be impatient, and always seem to be in a "time crunch."
3. They fear being taken advantage of.
4. They desire and seek change.
5. They like to do many things at once and become bored quickly.
6. They must be confronted or approached directly, because they respond best to direct communication.

Take a look at the Behavioral Tendencies, Strengths and Weaknesses of the **High "D," Dominant Director**, on the following page (Chart 4.1). Remember as you read these, that any strength overused has the potential to become a weakness.

High "D"—Dominant Director
chart of strengths and weaknesses

Strengths (General)	Weaknesses (General)
Strong-willed	Unsympathetic and cold
Productive	Insensitive and inconsiderate
Decisive	Cruel and sarcastic
Practical	Unforgiving
Visionary	Self-sufficient and domineering
Optimistic	Argumentative and impatient
Courageous	Opinionated and prejudiced
Born leader	Proud
Compulsive need for change	Crafty
Must correct wrongs	Can't relax
Not easily discouraged	Won't give up when losing
Independent and self-sufficient	Not complementary or emotional
Resolute	Impetuous

Strengths (With Spouse and Family)	Weaknesses (With Spouse and Family)
Exerts sound leadership	Tends to over dominate
Establishes goals	Too busy for family
Motivates family to action	Impatient with poor performance
Knows the right answer	Won't let children relax
Organizes household	Tends to use people
Has little need for friends	Too independent
Will work for group activity	Can't say "I'm sorry"
Excels in emergencies	May be right but unpopular
Goal-oriented	Low tolerance for error
Sees the whole picture	Doesn't analyze details
Organizes well	Is bored by the trivial
Seeks practical solutions	Is rash decision-maker
Moves quickly to action	Is rude or tactless
Delegates work	Is manipulative and demanding
Insists on production	Ends justify the means
Stimulates activity	Work may become his/her god
Thrives on opposition	Possessive

This chart was adapted from the Person to Person Certification Course by Sanford Kulkin, published by the Institute for Motivational Living, Inc.

THE DOMINANT DIRECTOR IN SCRIPTURE

Now that you know some of the characteristics of the Dominant Director ("D") personality style, let's get a little historical perspective. This personality style (and all others) has been around a long time!

The apostle Paul was a classic "D." His motto was, "I can do all things in Christ." Only a "D" could handle the confrontation Paul would encounter, plus the diverse environments he would face in opening up new fields for the gospel. And only a "D" would call a person a "hypocrite" publicly, as Paul did (Galatians 2:11-14).

Where an "I," "S," or "C" might have backed down when questioned by the Sanhedrin, Paul was bold and assertive. He took charge (Acts 22:30–23:3).

One of Paul's weaknesses was revealed when he refused to let Mark accompany him and Barnabas on a missionary journey—because Mark had abandoned their effort on their previous trip (Acts 15:36-38). In typical "D" style, Paul seemed to say, "Strike one: You're out! Mark, you're fired! Silas, you're hired. Let's go!"

Need another example of a Dominant Director in the Bible? If ever there was a "D," it was Sarah. Impatient in waiting for God's promise to give her and Abraham a son, she approached Abraham and *told* him, "Go sleep with my maidservant" (Genesis 16:1-2).

When Sarah felt she might lose control of the situation, she refused to admit her mistake and told Abraham, in essence, "You are responsible. Get rid of her" (Genesis 16:5). Her way was the best way, according to *Sarah*.

To her credit, Peter declares, "They were submissive to their own husbands, *like Sarah* who obeyed Abraham and called him master" (1 Peter 3:5-6). Somewhere along the way she learned she didn't always have to be in control. What an example for "D's" today!

THE COMMUNICATION STYLE OF THE DOMINANT DIRECTOR

As you just saw in the case of the apostle Paul, and in the story about Don and Donna at the beginning of this chapter, High "D's" are normally brief, direct, and to the point. They tend to ask "what" type questions. Because they desire results, high "D's" may be very focused in their questions and responses, particularly in their dealings with family members. They enjoy suggesting ways to achieve results, be in charge, and solve problems. This is especially true of the male Dominant Director. For example, he may have a tendency to cut his wife off in mid-sentence and offer suggestions for ways in which she can solve her problems or deal with situations. She, on the other hand, may not be looking for a solution. She needs to talk and relate to him. She needs for him to listen, not solve anything.

When the high "D" talks to you about ideas, he or she is usually quick to point out the logical benefits of those ideas or approaches. High "D's" expect us to agree with their ideas as well as with the facts they are presenting.

The Dominant Director will talk about problems in terms of how they may hamper accomplishment. "D's" tend to not be emotional in their approach. In fact, they may view an expression of emotion as a problem because it can slow things down. One high "D," when discussing finances with his wife, actually said, "I don't know why you find it necessary to waste time crying. We have a problem here and crying is not the solution!" You can well imagine how this affected their level of intimacy.

WHEN YOU ARE COMMUNICATING WITH DOMINANT DIRECTORS, REMEMBER NOT TO...

- **Ramble or repeat yourself.** This may make them feel as though you have something to hide, or are trying to take advantage of them.

- **Focus on problems.** They are results-oriented; they don't want to hear about problems, they want to hear about solutions and actions taken.

- **Be too sociable with them.** Even in an intimate setting, the high "D," male or female, has an agenda. If socialization is the goal of the interaction, they will initiate the "small talk" and be social. If they have another goal for the interaction, however, socialization may cause some frustration.

- **Make generalizations or make statements without supportive data.** While the "D" does not like detail, they do want the facts and benefits.

WHAT TO SAY TO "D'S"

Another thing to consider is that Dominant Directors may fail to adequately weigh the pros and cons. They tend to be impulsive and to ignore the potential risks of a situation. The high "D" will usually offer innovative and progressive systems and ideas or creative approaches to solving problems. "D's" rarely consider the opinions of others. They may be offended, however, if their advice is not followed.

Stuck for something to say? Here are some positive word pictures and "opening lines" that will be helpful in getting your communication with a Dominant Director spouse off on the right foot...

- "Your self-confidence is a turn-on to me."
- "You have a very forthright way of expressing yourself that I find fascinating."
- "You have such incredible tenacity when you have decided to go after something. I admire that."

- "I love the way you approach things you want with passion—including me!"
- "I know I can count on you to help me work things out."
- "I love your drive and determination to get things accomplished."
- "Changes don't seem to ruffle your feathers; you just adjust, adapt, and overcome."
- "I find your strong competitive spirit very exciting."
- "I enjoy the fact that you aren't afraid to try something new and go after it."

HIGH "D'S" AS LOVERS

In the home environment, the Dominant Director is decisive, independent, tries to maintain dominance, displays directness, and normally acts in a dynamic and strong-willed way to get what he or she wants. These individuals tend to carry those attitudes into their sexual behavior as well.

In typical high "D" fashion, Don's communication with Donna at the start of this chapter was brief, direct, and to the point. He was interested in determining the problem and getting it fixed. While such a style might work well in the workplace, accomplishing tasks that need to be completed, it is a terrible approach to lovemaking.

Sexual relationships were designed to be mutual interactions, not choreographed battlefields directed by a general. Don never seriously considered his wife's suggestions, or any thoughts she might have wanted to contribute about his role in their sexual difficulties.

Donna's greatest need, as it would be for most women (see Chapter Eight) was for him to *listen*, not solve the problem. His suggestions to increase her knowledge and possibly see a therapist could be helpful, but thrusting them upon her without her input was overwhelming and caused resentment. His approach and sarcastic comments made him appear cold and insensitive. People like Don tend to think the world revolves around their issues and needs. Black-and-white thinking contributes to seeing others as either for or against them—either right or wrong.

For Don and other male Dominant Director personalities, sex tends to be a rather self-focused personal goal. It may be used as an outlet for frustrations in other areas of life. The nuances of romance, let alone intimacy, can be lost on the high "D" male. He is certainly capable of being romantic, but oftentimes his motivation is to get what he wants. Consequently, his attempts at "romance" may be short-lived.

THE NEEDS OF THE DOMINANT DIRECTOR

Saying that "D's" need to be in control would be an understatement! A person with this style, depending on how high he or she tests on the intensity scale, has a tendency to try to decide for everyone. "D's" want to know everything that is happening and *why* these things are happening in twenty-five words or less. The intensity of their "D" determines how active and aggressive they will be in trying to overcome problems and obstacles.

Normally, it is accurate to say that the "D" factor measures the emotion of anger. In other words, the higher the "D," the quicker to become angry. High "D's" are the only personality style that actively seeks conflict as a means of controlling their environment. Remember, not only do they tend to perceive their environments as antagonistic, they prefer them that way.

"D's" believe that if they are moving, everyone around them should be moving as well. They may force a confrontation, especially with those styles that avoid it, simply to gain the upper hand and control the situation. Dominant Directors perceive some of the other personality styles as "weaker."

A high "D" male who allows his male ego to be in control can be a pretty tough person for the less aggressive styles to deal with. His idea of sexual foreplay might simply be the statement, "Brace yourself!" On the other hand, a high "D" female whose husband has a less active style may be perceived by him as the PMS poster girl.

The Dominant Director style needs to have a sense of authority, varied activities, prestige, freedom from controls, opportunities for personal growth, a "bottom line" approach, and an opportunity to achieve. "D's" enjoy achieving results, being in charge, and solving problems. Almost more than any other style, their internal radio dial is permanently set to station WII-FM (What's In It For Me?). Intimacy, therefore, must hold some excitement or be a pleasurable task.

When a problem exists, discuss it with your "D" in light of how it might hamper the status or movement of your relationship. Because of "D's" high ego strength, casting blame on them may exacerbate the situation. Focus on positive results and potential solutions, not just the problem.

BLIND SPOTS OF THE DOMINANT DIRECTOR

While it would not be fair to say that the high "D" personality tends to have more blind spots than any other style, it is true that they may be more prone to deny the existence of them. The higher the "D," the less effective they are at accepting the existence of their own ineffective behaviors. As a result, they tend at times to overuse their strengths to the point where those strengths become detrimental. There is a fine line here that is often blurred for the "D" style, because they are so strong-willed and focused. Pointing out blind spots to a Dominant Director is no easy task, but it can be done. Here are some ways to offer corrective feedback to Dominant Directors:

1. State the problem specifically, clearly, and concisely. Focus on the behavior, not on the "D" as a person. We love them; we dislike the behavior.

2. Suggest some positive action that can be taken as an alternative to the blind-spot behavior.

3. Let them know the positive results or benefits they can expect from taking the suggested action.

This is known as the PAR, or Problem-Action-Results, approach. It can be used with any of the personality styles but it is very successful in dealing with the high "D." Oh, one more hint. Don't come to them with a "laundry list" of problems and blind spots all at once. They process things better when they are offered in small doses. Remember, too, that since they don't like to be wrong, you may not gain instant acceptance. Be persistent but respectful in your approach.

HOW THE DOMINANT DIRECTOR IS TEMPTED

Male "D's" respond favorably to things that either build the male ego or fulfill male needs. They tend to be impulsive and quick to decide, often in the absence of detailed information. They enjoy "living on the edge," "pushing the limits," and "grabbing the gusto." Due to their natural tendency to become leaders, they often find themselves in situations where they are being sought after. Because they tend to perceive themselves as powerful people, they are tempted by sex, wealth, position, prestige, influence, admiration, control—in short, power. Their impulsiveness can lead to their downfall.

Female Dominant Directors, while not burdened with the additional problems brought about by the male ego, are still susceptible to many temptations resulting from their personality style and needs. For example, as a woman she needs affection. As a high "D," she demands it. She may be tempted, therefore, to find another source of affection when she is not receiving it from the expected source. This doesn't necessarily mean another man; it could simply involve another activity.

As is true with the high "D" male, control is intoxicating for the high "D" female as well. She just has a different "bent" toward it than he does. A high "D" female whose husband is a more passive style, may find the biblical role of submission to her spouse almost unbearable. She may cry out, "He won't move...He can't decide...He doesn't seem to care if or when things get done...He has no ambition! How can I be submissive if he won't take the lead?" In this situation, the temptation to seize control is sometimes overwhelming for the "D" woman.

It's hard for others outside of these circumstances to understand the feelings of a woman who may be gifted in running things, yet she has chosen to take a subordinate position. Open and honest communication between the husband and wife needs to be focused on moving both parties toward a center of balance. The husband may need to take some calculated steps toward being more decisive. The wife, on the other hand, may need to practice detaching herself from the tasks at hand.

THE DOMINANT DIRECTOR'S VIEWPOINTS ON SEX

For the male Dominant Director, sex is another goal to be achieved. That goal normally centers around the sex act and his own orgasm. Usually, his attempts at "romance" are short-lived and end once the goal has been achieved. He may also have a tendency to focus on his own physical performance sexually, while partially or totally ignoring his partner's needs.

High "D" males may use sex as an outlet for frustrations they are feeling in other areas of their lives. This only tends to intensify their "conquest" orientation. High "D's" can be great lovers if that is their goal. Since they have high ego strength, they just might want to be the best. If the Dominant Director decides to put romance and intimacy at the top of the priority list, life can get very exciting for his or her partner.

The high "D" female may be assertive when it comes to sex, initiating the action. Again, this could lead to some frustration if her husband is a more passive type. Even males with passive personality styles have a male ego.

When the woman becomes the sexual aggressor, some males may feel threatened. As a result, they may withdraw affection, or simply withdraw altogether. Other males may enjoy the sexually aggressive female, but they may become frustrated when they want intimacy and she does not take the lead. On the other hand, in an atmosphere of trust and open communication, the high "D" female will have very positive sexual viewpoints. She doesn't mind new and different experiences and will lead the way—if and when she feels loved.

HINTS FOR HELPING THE DOMINANT DIRECTOR RELATE TO ANOTHER DOMINANT DIRECTOR

The keys to making this relationship work center around common goals. If there is mutual respect in the relationship, the high "D" will tend to see another high "D" as driving, visionary, assertive, aggressive, competitive, and optimistic. If you and your spouse have a common goal, there is little doubt you will accomplish it together. However, should mutual respect be absent, or the goal focus differs, the relationship will rapidly deteriorate into a battle for control. In this situation, you may view each other as argumentative, dictatorial, arrogant, domineering, nervous, or hasty.

In a nutshell—*Mutual respect must exist for conflict to be avoided and intimacy to flourish. Both people need to understand each other's expectations concerning intimacy, sexual parameters, roles, and boundaries.*

HINTS FOR HELPING THE DOMINANT DIRECTOR RELATE TO THE INFLUENCER

If you are a "D," you may view the high "I" as egocentric, superficial, overly optimistic, glib, too self-assured, and inattentive. Because of your own high ego strength, you may feel threatened by someone who seems to be so secure with herself or himself. In fact, "I's" may appear to be "in love" with themselves. Why? Because they like to talk, talk, talk. About what? Themselves! Remember, they need to have some time to socialize before they "get down to business."

You also may be somewhat put off by the fact that "I's" seem to be constantly "selling" themselves. If you're spending your time with them, you've already bought, right? Wrong! Don't forget that the "I's" greatest fear is a loss of your approval and rejection; "I's" need reassurance that you are continuing to buy. The high "I" does not like to lose, and is concerned with how to let you win. If you win and it makes you happy, they are sure you will "like" them. They perceive that as a win for them.

"I's" are concerned with making their partners happy in a sexual relationship to gain their approval. Because of this "win/win" philosophy, they may be a bit hesitant to express their dissatisfaction or individual needs. Stretch yourself and talk to your "I" partner about intimacy. Give him or her some time to build rapport with you and gain assurance that you are your Influencer's best friend, as well as lover.

In a nutshell—*Once you draw "I's" out in conversation, be friendly, complimentary, listen to their ideas, and listen to the feelings they are expressing. Build them up, because they want to please you.*

HINTS FOR HELPING THE DOMINANT DIRECTOR RELATE TO THE STEADY RELATOR

A high "D" may view high "S's" as impassive, nonchalant, apathetic, accepting, possessive, complacent, and non-demonstrative. Because your "S's" greatest fear is losing security or feeling insecure, your direct "D" style may be a bit overwhelming to him or her. Bear in mind that he or she dislikes confrontation and will go to great lengths to avoid it. As a result, your "S" may fall silent or withdraw from you. Hard as it may be, don't follow your natural instinct to pursue or badger. That will only make an "S" more steadfast and determined to turn inward and get away from you.

The best thing to do in dealing with Steady Relators is to allow them time and space. They respond to secure feelings about the relationship and interaction. This occurs by touching, hugging, and communicating in a soft, loving tone. Once you have approached them in this way, they will voluntarily open up to you.

Another thing you may notice about high "S's"—they tend to be slow moving. Just remember, a microwave may heat food up quickly, but a crock pot allows the flavors to blend together slowly, producing a much higher quality of taste. There are advantages to slow and steady as well as to quick and hot. Learn to appreciate their pace.

"D's" adapt to change rather quickly while "S's" need to process it. Try to avoid "springing" things on "S's" at the last minute—especially sex. However, you can spring a loving dose of kindness on them any time you want. Often, they may exhibit outward agreement with you but inwardly be resisting if you are pressing them for sex. They may comply with their body, but their heart and soul are not there.

In a nutshell—*Avoid pressuring "S's." Recognize their need for intimacy, be friendly, softer, more easygoing, and "throttle back" your pace to slow and steady. Try setting your internal microwave on "defrost" rather than "turbo cook," and see what happens.*

HINTS FOR HELPING THE DOMINANT DIRECTOR RELATE TO THE CONSCIENTIOUS THINKER

If you are a "D," dealing with the high "C" may present your greatest challenge. This is because you may see them as overly dependent on their systematic approach to life. You may see them as evasive, defensive, too focused on details, and too cautious and worrisome. However, they, like you, are also task/goal-oriented.

They just value the "process" of accomplishing the task and reaching the goal almost as much as they do the goal itself. Let's suppose you have an operable brain tumor.

Consider for a moment the personality of your surgeon. The goal or task is to remove the tumor, right? However, in this case, the process of removing it is just as critical. Would you prefer a surgeon who is going to "just go in there and get that sucker out," or one who will study the X-rays, do a CAT scan, plan the least damaging route, and fully brief you on the risks and benefits?

You might answer, "Building relationships is not brain surgery." Well, you're right. But if you don't take the time to do either one of them right, you could end up with a serious headache!

You may perceive that your high "C" has a tendency to over-analyze things and get bogged down in details. It's true that he or she sometimes suffers from the "paralysis of analysis." Because "C's" fear criticism, their avoidance behavior centers around "doing it right." From their perspective, no one can criticize perfection. While you may be concerned with "getting it done," they are concerned with "getting it done right." When you think about it, there really isn't a lot of difference.

In a nutshell—*As with the high "S," try to slow down the pace. Give "C's" lots of information in a clear format and provide as many details and facts as possible. Be prepared for the doubts, concerns, and questions they may express about the ideas you have, or about your motives. They are not "nit-picking," they are simply clarifying. They need assurance that you are not manipulating them. Try to develop a nonthreatening approach and allow them time to react to you intimately. Don't overly pressure them or force a confrontation, because they will withdraw affection, rather than give affection to make peace.*

PERSONAL AREAS OF GROWTH FOR THE DOMINANT DIRECTOR

Finally, since nobody's perfect, you'll want to consider some ways you can make adjustments to your personal style. If you are a "D"...

- **Try not to control or dominate the situation, the conversation, or the other person.** Strive to be an "active" listener. Focus on what others are saying, as well as how it is being said and the feelings they are expressing.
- **Put more energy into personal relationships.** Show your support for your spouse and children by investing your time, attention, and self.
- **Slow down! Take time to explain the "whys" behind your statements and requests.** Don't be so fast-paced or goal-oriented. Talk and move a bit slower. Tone it down.

- **Be more open in sharing your feelings.** Also, strive to be more approachable so others can share their feelings with you.
- **Practice patience and listen until you understand your spouse's feelings, ideas, suggestions, and requests.** Don't butt in, give advise, or criticize. Just listen, listen, listen. Give others the opportunity to catch up with you. Be affirming, because they may feel less intelligent, weak, less confident, and simply inadequate if you exhibit impatience.
- **Take a good look at your blind spots.** Allow God to give you eyes to see and ears to hear.

CHAPTER FIVE

The Influencer

Isabella gathered up her laundry in one hand and the box of lasagna she had picked up from Pasta-To-Go with the other. She kicked the car door shut with her foot and was nearly breathless when she pushed open the screen door and dashed into the kitchen.

"I'm so sorry I'm late, Ivan," she said without missing a beat, "I had more errands than I thought. And wouldn't you know I ran into everyone…just, everyone! It always happens when you're in a hurry. Did you know Mrs. Leflander has been in the hospital? I must take her some flowers. And Gayle—well, you know Gayle—she had to tell me every detail of her son Johnny's new job. The time was rolling by but she is such a sweet lady, I just couldn't cut her off. How are you, honey? I'll have dinner in a flash…I just need to clear a place here at the counter…I'm sorry, I intended to get this project finished today; I know the mess has been bothering you and I promised…but they needed an extra hand down at the church this morning."

Ivan smiled and kindly didn't say anything. Isabella was, well, Isabella—full of energy and conversation, friendly, and generous of time and attention. Occasionally he wished a little more was directed toward him. But on the whole, he had few complaints—especially in the bedroom. Their sex life was extraordinary.

"Ivan," she would purr, "there's a full moon tonight and the balcony beckons..." Isabella was a creative and willing partner when she wasn't distracted and overextended by her many involvements. Occasionally the mood would be lost when she started telling him about something and then forget to stop. But she had been known to greet him at the door with nothing on but a trench coat.

The biggest turn-on for Ivan, however, was the fact that Isabella never failed to compliment him on his skill and sensitivity as a lover. "You know exactly what to do with your hands," she would whisper in his ear. If things didn't turn out as planned sexually, as occasionally happens in all relationships, she was quick to take the blame and apologize. Sometimes Ivan wondered if she wasn't a little too ready to try and set things right. She really hated the times when he was cross with her, and she would plunge into a major funk if his mood lasted for any length of time.

Living with Isabella was a challenge, but it was never, ever boring.

UNDERSTANDING THE INFLUENCER

The Influencer personality style is characterized by active, positive movement through what they perceive as a favorable environment. Basically, this means that when they view the environment as positive, they seek to enjoy themselves in it.

The greatest fear of the Influencer is loss of social approval and/or rejection. Influencers, therefore, will make every attempt to "win people over" or influence others to like and approve of them. They are extremely people-oriented and are often quite charismatic. They love to talk. And "I's" tend to be optimistic, almost to a fault. They strive to find the fun, or the good, in every situation and every person they meet.

To help you recognize the high "I," here is a quick reference list of their most common characteristics:

1. They tend to be emotional people who "wear their heart on their sleeve." They react emotionally, and often dramatically, to situations and people.

2. People-oriented is an understatement. The high "I" loves being with other people; the more the merrier. They are very demonstrative in their dealings with others.

3. They fear losing the approval of others.

4. High "I's" tend to be disorganized. Keeping up with details, following things through, and being on time are not their strong suits.

5. High "I's" are optimistic. Because of their environmental view point, they tend to see the world as a "user-friendly" place. They strive to find the "silver lining" in every cloud.

6. High "I" people are great encouragers. They flatter you, agree with you, and make great cheerleaders.

Because of these and the many other admirable qualities of the high "I," they are great people to be around. They desire to associate with others like them, and, as a rule, they are very accepting of change and variety. About eleven percent of the population is comprised of Influencers. Fortunately for their spouses, their upbeat, adventurous attitudes carry over into their sex lives.

The strengths and weaknesses of the **High "I," Influencer,** are listed in the chart on the following page. As we said before, any strength overused has the potential to become a weakness.

INFLUENCERS IN THE SCRIPTURES

In the Bible, Peter illustrates the Influencer personality style well. He's a talker! So much so, that more is recorded about what he said than about what the rest of the disciples said. The word *impetuous* fits Peter, who was always ready to jump into a conversation with an answer like, "Lord, I will lay my life down for you."

High "I"—Influencer
chart of strengths and weaknesses

Strengths (General)	Weaknesses (General)
Outgoing and charismatic	Undisciplined and weak-willed
Warm and friendly	Restless and Naive
Talkative, "life of the party"	Disorganized and Unproductive
Compassionate and demonstrative	Undependable
Generous and sincere at heart	Egocentric
Good sense of humor	Exaggerates and is compulsive talker
Has memory for stories	Fearful and insecure
Enthusiastic and expressive	Dwells on trivia
Good on stage	Egotistical and obnoxious
Wide-eyed and innocent	Controlled by circumstances
Lives in the present	Gets angry easily
Changeable disposition	Seems phony to some

Strengths (Spouse and Family)	Weaknesses (Spouse and Family)
Is liked by children's friends	Keeps home in a frenzy
Turns disaster into humor	Is disorganized and forgetful
Is the circus-master	Doesn't listen to the whole story
Thrives on compliments	Dominates conversations
Is envied by others	Answers for others
Apologizes quickly	Can be fickle
Likes spontaneous activities	Makes excuses
Volunteers for jobs	Would rather talk than work
Thinks up new activities	Forgets obligations
Looks great on the surface	Doesn't follow through
Is creative and colorful	Confidence fades fast
Has energy and enthusiasm	Is undisciplined
Starts in a flashy way	Priorities are out of order
Inspires others to join	Decides by feelings
Charms others to work	Easily distracted
	Wastes time talking
	Scares others off at times

This chart was adapted from the Person to Person Certification Course by Sanford Kulkin, published by the Institute for Motivational Living, Inc. (C) 1983, All rights reserved. Used by Permission.

Oh, really? Afraid of losing approval and fearful of rejection, Peter later lies, "I don't know what you're talking about," when a servant girl claims he was one of those who followed Jesus Christ.

Enthusiasm and optimism ran rampant in Peter. Only an "I" would enthusiastically jump from a boat and swim to the shore, optimistically shouting, "It's the Lord! It's the Lord!" (John 21:7).

Looking for another "I"? Take a look at Rebekah. Abraham's servant goes off looking for a wife for Abraham's son, Isaac, and meets Rebekah. Does she make an impression on this servant? Does she ever! She gives him water that she draws from the well, she waits and then feeds the man's camels, and, with the people-centeredness of an "I," she invites the servant to spend the night in her father's house. To top it all off, she tells him his livestock will be cared for, as well.

Believe me, only an Influencer would leave home with a man she had just met, to marry a man she was yet to meet. Talk about optimism! (You can read the story of Rebekah in Genesis 24.)

THE COMMUNICATION STYLE OF THE INFLUENCER

Let's get back to our discussion of present-day Influencers. Like other high "I's," Isabella, mentioned earlier in this chapter, enjoyed establishing a candid and friendly environment for communication with others. Such openness will help her feel approved and loved. Influencer personality types like nothing better than talking about, planning, and visualizing their various projects—sometimes they would rather talk about them than act. Verbalizing ideas and sharing intuition about and with others is exciting within and apart from the bedroom. As with Isabella, details might be overlooked. The high "I" may interrupt to share an idea, but problem-solving is creative, and new ways are sought to accomplish routine tasks, making them exciting and fun.

Ivan enjoyed being around Isabella. Influencers tend to be in the spotlight, and those "I's" who keep their strengths in balance are perceived as ambitious, stimulating, enthusiastic, dramatic, and fun to be around.

"I's" can, however, have big emotional outbursts if stressed. When this happens, they may be viewed by others as manipulative, over excitable, undisciplined, and egotistical. The fear of not being loved and accepted can be hidden by the "I's" outgoing and gregarious ways, but it is always lurking near the surface. Sexual behavior and preferences, intimacy, and sexual performance are especially sensitive areas for Influencers because when they do not meet expectations, they feel they are unworthy or unlovable.

The Influencer will invariably try to establish a favorable, friendly environment. He or she needs to have an opportunity to verbalize ideas, discuss these ideas with other people, and share his or her intuition. The high "I" may get so wrapped up in talking about something that he or she fails to transfer what has been verbalized into action.

"I's" enjoy hearing stories and testimonials about other people. A vital part of the high "I's" communication style revolves around stimulating sociable activities. They tend to skip over details and get bored quickly when dealing with or dwelling on details. In fact, if you want to make sure that the high "I" gets the details, it would be best to communicate the details to them in writing.

The high "I" loves to share information in the context of a participative relationship. For example, he or she may press for dialogue in a confrontational situation. This can be a problem when "I's" are dealing with the less assertive styles who prefer to withdraw and process information, rather than confront and verbalize.

WHEN COMMUNICATING WITH THE INFLUENCER, BE SURE YOU...

- Allow some time for socialization and "small talk."
- Try not to monopolize the conversation, structure the interaction, or control the pace.
- Acknowledge their ideas and accomplishments. Say something positive about how they look or what they've done. Let them know they have your approval.
- Never "tell" them what to do. Always try to ask or solicit from them what they think (for men) or what they feel (for women) should be done. Give them time to verbally develop and explain their solution, action plan, idea, or concept.

WHAT TO SAY TO "I'S"

In the process of analyzing information, Influencers may lose concentration. They are easily distracted because they don't want to "miss" anything, and as a result, they may not absorb important facts or details. They may interrupt you to share an idea of their own.

The high "I" is generally a creative problem-solver. He or she looks for new ways to do routine tasks and make things exciting and fun. Here are some "opening lines" and word pictures which are guaranteed to break the ice when communicating with an Influencer...

- "I really admire people with a good sense of humor like yours."
- "You certainly have a good command of the language."
- "You're very observant. I could not help but notice how you picked up on everything that was going on around you."
- "You remind me of the Energizer bunny. When I'm around you, I get charged up!"
- "You are really gifted at motivating people. You could sell an air conditioner to an Eskimo in January."
- "You never cease to amaze me."
- "You paint with words the way Michaelangelo painted with a brush."

INFLUENCERS AS LOVERS

In short, sex usually is great with the high "I." Why? Because he or she doesn't want to be rejected. Isabella risked offering some creative (some might say *outrageous)* propositions in order to please Ivan. His acceptance and delight with her enabled her to feel good about herself.

Isabella's nearly insatiable need for communication means Ivan must be willing to talk, share, and listen. If he is the strong, silent type, feelings of insecurity might be triggered in Isabella, for she would have no feedback on where she stands with him. If he is another Influencer, their sexual communication is apt to be superior because they will be motivated to talk about what each needs for sexual satisfaction. There is only one caveat for two Influencers—they may talk so much that they forget to make love!

THE NEEDS OF THE INFLUENCER

Besides loving to talk, high "I" people also tend to be emotional and somewhat dramatic, or even flamboyant, in their manner. For example, they may enjoy making an "entrance," and often arrive just a bit late. They need to be noticed and admired. They like everyone; why shouldn't everyone like them?

When in an antagonistic environment, the Influencer will respond actively and may try to negotiate some type of agreement. However, "I's" don't like confrontation and will try to avoid situations that may become confrontational. They tend to be diplomatic in their approach, and they enjoy the art of win/win negotiation. Extremely high "I" people are joyful and optimistic. They need to be social, and a high "I" female has a deep need to spend time just talking and relating to her husband.

If your spouse is a high "I," it may be something of a burden for him or her to be responsible for handling the finances, or balancing the check book. "What do you mean I'm overdrawn? I still have checks left, I must have more money!" Mundane details are not the "I's" forte.

BLIND SPOTS OF THE INFLUENCER

When Influencers keep their strengths in balance, they are perceived as being friendly, outgoing, pleasant, and entertaining. However, they tend to have major emotional reactions and outbursts when pushed too far. Their words can fly like bullets from a machine gun, and be just as damaging. This will cause the other styles to run for cover. Influencers sometimes develop their strengths to such an extent that they become weaknesses. When this happens, "I's" can be viewed by others as manipulative, excitable, undisciplined, and egotistical. They seem to be saying, "Galileo was wrong; the world revolves around me!"

Because of their fear of rejection, it can really be a challenge to present these blind spots to your Influencer. One thing you will want to do for sure is take time to build a favorable, friendly environment in which he or she feels comfortable and not threatened.

Give him or her the opportunity to verbalize. While "I's" are analyzing information, they may lose concentration or miss important facts and details. You may want to get your "I" focused on what you are going to say before you say it. Then try and tie the blind spot to a positive behavior, or offer an alternative positive behavior in its place. Be specific and brief about the blind spot; don't dwell on it. Take time to expand on the alternative positive behavior and give your "I" the opportunity to share his or her ideas with you regarding it.

If the conversation revolves around sexual behavior, preferences, intimacy, or performance, it is particularly important for you to stress strengths. The more personal the subject, the more gently it needs to be introduced to the "I." Even though Influencers may be outgoing and gregarious, never forget their greatest fear—rejection. "I's" are prone to be a bit insecure about themselves, although they cover up these feelings quite well with their demonstrative manner. Your Influencer needs constant reassurance that he or she is terrific and loved by others—most of all, by you.

HOW THE INFLUENCER IS TEMPTED

Let me count the ways! Because they are positive and active, the high "I" is attracted to people and activities that are fun, exciting, interesting, flashy, spontaneous, fashionable, accepted by peers, and popular. All these provide "I's" with good feelings about themselves.

Influencers as children don't want to go to bed because they are afraid they will miss something! In fact, one of the "I's" greatest attributes as an adult is a childlike approach to life, and a sense of excitement they bring to everything they do. And with childlike abandon, they want to be free of many rules and regulations. "I's" tend to be very spontaneous people who respond well to verbal persuasion.

Their passionate attitudes about life and the desire to live it to the fullest can make "I's," without other mediating factors, susceptible to people, settings, or situations where sexual involvement with someone other than their spouse could occur. Flattery, praise, regard, and unconditional acceptance attract and can tempt them.

THE INFLUENCER'S VIEWPOINTS ON SEX

An extremely high "I" may subscribe to the sexual philosophy, "If it feels good, do it!" A male Influencer with his male ego in full operation may use the strengths of his personality style to achieve his goal of having sex. Because he is fulfilling his need to be physically desirable by being demonstrative, he gladly meets the female's need for touch. His communication skills, which are normally fine-tuned, powerfully appeal to a female's need for relationship, listening, and talking. A male "I" will intuitively say the right things at the right time to help a woman feel more secure.

The female Influencer, on the other hand, has a need for affection that is going to be met through verbal expression. For her, sex is part of the total picture of the relationship, not the object of it. For example, she needs her partner to spend time listening to her. For the female high "I," the emotional and relational aspects surrounding sex are of paramount concern.

Where other styles may have some difficulty expressing their feelings about sex, as a general rule the high "I" will be much more comfortable. Of course, their degree of openness depends on the level of acceptance that their partner is demonstrating. Because of this bent toward openness, two high "I's" will probably have a terrific and active sex life.

HINTS FOR HELPING THE INFLUENCER RELATE TO ANOTHER INFLUENCER

The Influencer will view another high "I" as stimulating, charismatic, outgoing, and optimistic. The two will develop a relationship quickly and relate well to each other, often feeling a tremendous sense of "chemistry." They may compete for recognition at times, and will strive to impress one another, but they will both try to please.

Intimacy is easy for two Influencers because they have no secrets from one another and have learned to say the "right" things. They both strive for admiration and will go to great extremes to provide the other with a satisfying experience.

Intimacy is usually maintained, since they are avoiding confrontation and rejection.

In a nutshell—*If you are a high "I" in love with another high "I," be friendly, complimentary, and acknowledge your partner's accomplishments. Listen sincerely to what he or she is saying, instead of planning your own next lines.*

HINTS FOR HELPING THE INFLUENCER RELATE TO THE DOMINANT DIRECTOR

The high "I" may see the Dominant Director as argumentative, dictatorial, arrogant, domineering, nervous, and hasty. Why? Because normally the high "D" is focused on task accomplishment and doesn't want to take the time to socialize. Developing intimacy with him or her is not always easy. When this happens, the high "I" feels rejected and may see the high "D" as undesirable. The "I" may then look for a more receptive environment.

The high "I" may resent being "told" what to do sexually, which is often the high "D's" approach. The "I" would do what is asked just to please if the "D" would engage in meaningful conversation. The Influencer prefers to be asked not only to do something, but to have an opportunity to share his or her ideas, opinions, or methods about how to do whatever is desired.

The high "I" can be easily offended by the Dominant Director's autocratic tendencies, because "I's" prefer to be more participative. They don't just want to "do," they want to experience "doing" with and for others. In addition, high "D's" are interested in what they perceive as the end result of intimacy. In the process, they may ignore the feelings the Influencer is trying to express. This makes the high "I" feel as though he or she is being rejected.

An "I" may resort to trying to "charm" the high "D," only to become confused or frustrated when he or she does not receive a favorable response. At that point the "I" may become discouraged and give up. This does not need to happen. In dealing with the Dominant Director, the Influencer can capitalize on his or her ability to verbalize feelings by presenting them directly and succinctly.

Avoid over verbalizing or beating around the bush! To your high "D," this is like wearing a sport coat made of raw liver into a den of hungry Pit Bulls. This is especially true if the issue at hand is something of a personal one to your Dominant Director. Instead, discuss his or her commitment to the relationship in terms of mutual satisfaction and benefits. Prepare your thoughts before the interaction. Influencers can relieve their intense need to verbalize by rehearsing and editing what they are going to say ahead of time.

Remember, high "D's" don't like to hear about relational problems; they want you to be satisfied with the way things are. In fact, they would prefer to hear that there are no problems. Without confronting them on issues of intimacy immediately, you run the risk of having them say something like, "Why are you telling me this now? I thought you were happy!" Of course, Influencers needs to overcome their fear of rejection and get these things out on the table right away.

In a nutshell—*Be brief, direct, and to the point about your concerns. Don't expect the "D" to "read between the lines." A good approach is to ask "what" and "how" type questions. Highlight the logical relational benefits of an intimate relationship. When a problem exists, discuss it immediately, with love and respect.*

HINTS FOR HELPING THE INFLUENCER RELATE TO THE STEADY RELATOR

The Influencer has a tendency to think that the Steady Relator is impassive, nonchalant, apathetic, possessive, complacent, nondemonstrative, and maybe even a bit boring. This is really a matter of pacing. The Steady Relator has a tendency to move a bit slower and more methodically than the Influencer.

Influencers, who are happiest when they are moving so fast that their hair catches fire, can be somewhat put off by the slower pace of the high "S." This may affect intimacy because the "I" may perceive the absence of instant acceptance as rejection. In reality, the high "S" is simply "processing" through the situation in an attempt to feel more secure. However, the high "I" may lose patience when the high "S" does not react quickly and may begin to try and convince the "S." This makes the "S" feel even more insecure.

On the other hand, under the right circumstances, the Influencer can be a motivator and encourager to the high "S." One of the pitfalls here, however, is that the high "I" will become frustrated when the high "S" does not verbally express his or her thoughts and feelings. The Steady Relator, for example, withdraws verbalization and affection from the high "I" who is pressing to "talk it over."

What you have here is a Badger trying to open a Clam. The harder the Influencer tries to get the high "S" to talk about something, the more determined the Steady Relator is to withdraw by "clamming up." The "S" may want to talk about intimate things, but can't get the "I" to be quiet long enough to really hear what he or she has to say.

It would be to the Influencer's benefit, when dealing with the Steady Relator, to slow down just a bit. Try to be a little more easygoing, and *listen*. Be specific and sincere in showing your appreciation. Work at establishing a genuine friendship with your high "S." Bear in mind that because of his or her style, the word "friend" has a very special meaning to Steady Relators. They don't build intimate relationships quickly or lightly. They build relationships based on trust, over a long period of time.

"S's" are concerned with substance, not flash. You will not convince them to have sex or intimacy with you until you get them to enter a process which leads to intimacy.

In a nutshell—*You should have no trouble creating a favorable environment which is personal and romantic. Express genuine love and affection toward Steady Relators and be patient in drawing out their inner feelings. Listen, listen, listen! Don't be pushy, overly aggressive, demanding, or confrontational.*

HINTS FOR HELPING THE INFLUENCER RELATE TO THE CONSCIENTIOUS THINKER

Perhaps the greatest relational challenge for the Influencer is building intimacy with the high "C." Influencers view the high "C" as overly dependent on systems, evasive, defensive, too focused on details, and too cautious or worrisome. In fact, the Influencer may feel somewhat frustrated, and may avoid intimacy with the high "C" because, from the "I's" perspective, the "C" tends to get bogged down in details, and wants everything perfect before intimacy can take place.

The high "I" perceives that the "C" lacks spontaneity and appears to be looking for the hidden meanings in things. An "I" may feel that a "C" is always looking for something "wrong" with him or her, and therefore cannot measure up to the "C's" expectations: "I'm just not perfect enough." This will cause the high "I" to feel rejected. The Influencer is focused on pleasing his or her partner in the relationship, while the "C" is focused on the partner's actions. This incompatible view and orientation is a major cause for relational stress for these two styles. The "I" views intimacy with a less critical eye than the "C."

It would be helpful for the "I" to keep track of intimate fires that the "C" has smothered with criticism or the removal of affection. This information must be presented in a nonthreatening and positive way, without anger. When disagreeing, be sure that the disagreement is over facts and not about personality. Discussion should take place without a lot of emotion. Try not to be defensive or argumentative. When providing explanations, be diplomatic, patient, and persistent. The Conscious Thinker needs to be convinced by the quality, relevance, and sincerity of what is being said, not by the quantity of words.

In a nutshell—*Respect the "C's" need for attending to details and deepness of thought. High "C's" want a controlled and predictable environment, so avoid "springing" things on him or her. "C's" are hard on themselves, so they need to have positive things said to them, in addition to being reassured and knowing exactly what to expect. Slow down your pace. Explain, listen, and address the "C's" concerns with sincerity. Weigh your words very carefully. Conscientious thinkers get their feelings hurt easily and do not forget.*

PERSONAL AREAS OF GROWTH FOR THE INFLUENCER

You may want to think about making some positive adjustments to your high "I" style, in order to fit into the lives of others more comfortably. Here are a few suggestions, if you are an "I..."

- **Curb your natural impulsiveness.** Spend a bit more time weighing the pros and cons of a situation before making a decision.
- **Work toward being more results-oriented.** Exercise control over your actions, words, and emotions.
- **Talk a little less, listen a little more.** Remember to match the pace of your partner, even if it means slowing down a lot.
- **Concentrate on following through with tasks and commitments.** Focus more on details, names, organization, and facts.
- **Consider and evaluate your partner's ideas and suggestions and use them in preference to your own whenever possible.** Be more sensitive to the interests of others.
- **Use your creativity to find ways to keep the relationship vital.** Find exciting ways to draw your partner out. Remember, they were attracted to you because you are "fun."

CHAPTER SIX

The Steady Relator

Steve watched out the window as his wife Susan and their son slipped into the van to go rent a movie for their Friday night family night. While Steve wasn't the type to say much about his devotion to Susan, the look on his face would have announced to anyone watching that he adored her.

Perhaps it was the fire in the fireplace, or the rain running down the window, making its intricate patterns of little rivers, that made him feel so nostalgic. His shoulders shivered a bit as he thought how close he had come to missing all of this. While he had been stunned by Susan's outgoing nature and grounded view of life from the moment he met her, he had been slow to do anything about it.

Steve was a hard-working, in-the-background kind of guy who quietly took care of business. It had taken him three months to ask Susan out. When she said yes, he'd been terrified, but they'd had a great time—Steve could listen to her for hours—and she laughed at all his corny jokes. They dated for over three years. While Steve knew almost from the beginning that he wanted to marry Susan, he just never got around to saying so.

Steve was shocked when Susan gave him an ultimatum to make their situation permanent or say good-bye. At first Steve was stubborn and determined not to be pushed (after three years) into anything. However, within a week he had moved into an indecisive and fearful mode. After two more weeks, he was totally panicked at the prospect of losing her.

Susan was disappointed that Steve chose to be such a spectator concerning the wedding plans, but everything was lovely, and in the end Steve seemed pleased. Indeed, Steve was very happy. Marriage provided stability and an emotional connection that was immensely satisfying to him. Susan refused to let his life get dull, but it was the familiarity of their day-by-day living that he appreciated most.

If there was any area of discontent for Steve, it was their sexual relationship. Here Steve's laid-back style was less tolerable to Susan. He underestimated the amount of energy and planning—work if you will—that was needed to make a sexual relationship satisfying. He failed to set aside time for special dates and quiet moments alone with his wife. Fearful of pushing himself on her, he backed off from sex if he felt she wasn't totally enthusiastic.

Steve's fear of overstepping and forcing himself on Susan was interpreted by her as lack of interest. Steve loved having a family—he would avoid or go along with almost anything so as not to "upset the apple cart." But his tendency to go with the flow and his failure to communicate openly and honestly was undermining the peace he sought. He and Susan had almost stopped having sex without saying a word about it.

UNDERSTANDING THE STEADY RELATOR

High "S" people like Steve truly enjoy simple pleasures of life. Their approach to relationships is focused on the person they love and on the feelings they derive from that person. Their greatest fear is a loss of security.

Since "S's" move by their feelings, if they don't feel good about doing something, they won't do it. Even if they do, their heart won't be in it and they'll simply go through the motions without the emotions. Because "S's" are in touch with their feelings, their intuition about situations and people seems to be finely tuned.

Here are some other things you can expect from Steady Relators…

1. They are loyal, gentle, and prefer being part of a team, unit, group, or family.

2. They strive to be persons of substance. They need to be trustworthy and appreciated, and they do things for others out of relationship, not obligation.

3. They fear a loss of status quo.
4. The high "S" person tends to be family-oriented. He or she wants to preserve the family unit and marriage at all costs.
5. "S's" display a high level of trust, compassion, and sympathy toward others. They try to maintain high levels of competence, and they tend to be peacemakers.
6. In their attempts to maintain their security and the status quo, "S's" may be viewed as possessive or stubborn.
7. They tend to resist change and adapt to it slowly.
8. "S's" have lots of "common sense."

The Steady Relator style is the most prevalent of the four styles, which only tends to reinforce the fact that God is infinite in His wisdom regarding each and every detail of creation. Please don't misunderstand: It's not that we think this one style is better than another. However, can you imagine what things might be like if, for example, sixty-nine percent of people displayed Dominant Director tendencies? God is seriously concerned with maintaining balance, isn't He?

Please refer to the adjacent chart to see the general and relational characteristics of the **High "S," Steady Relator.** Remember, as with all other personality types, strengths can become weaknesses if carried to the extreme.

High "S"—Steady Relator
chart of strengths and weaknesses

Strengths (General)	Weaknesses (General)
Likable and diplomatic	Unmotivated and blasé
Efficient and organized	Spectator
Dependable	Selfish and stubborn
Conservative and practical	Stingy
Reluctant leader	Self-protective
Low-key personality	Indecisive and fearful
Easygoing and relaxed	Unenthusiastic
Patient and well-balanced	Reticent
Quiet but witty	Avoids responsibility
Sympathetic and kind	Quiet will of iron
Keeps emotions hidden	Too compromising
Happily reconciled to life	Self-righteous

Strengths (Spouse and Family)	Weaknesses (Spouse and Family)
Makes a good parent	Is undisciplined and unchangeable
Is not in a hurry	Doesn't organize the home
Can take the good with the bad	Takes life too easy
Doesn't get upset easily	Dampens others' enthusiasm
Is pleasant and enjoyable	Stays uninvolved
Good listener, compassionate	Indifferent to plans
Dry sense of humor	Judges others
Has several close friends	Is sarcastic and teasing
Competent and steady	Not goal-oriented
Peaceful and agreeable	Lacks self-motivation
Has administrative ability	Is hard to get moving
Mediates problems	Resents being pushed
Avoids conflicts	Is lethargic and careless
Good under pressure	Discourages others
Finds the easy way	Is an observer

This chart was adapted from the Person to Person Certification Course by Sanford Kulkin, published by the Institute for Motivational Living, Inc.

THE STEADY RELATOR IN THE SCRIPTURES

If you ever want to meet an "S" in the Bible, read about Father Abraham. A Steady Relator start to finish. At our first glimpse of him in Genesis, his extreme loyalty to family is clear when he leaves Mesopotamia. Despite the command of the Lord to leave his family behind, Abraham takes his nephew, Lot, to Canaan with him. Later, when Sarah orders Abraham to sleep with her Egyptian maidservant, he acquiesces—a classic "S" surrender to a domineering spouse. Sometime after that, after Sarah bore Abraham a son, Isaac, Sarah tells Abraham to send away the maidservant and her son. Unwilling to confront Sarah ("S's" avoid confrontation at all costs), Abraham does what he is told and sends Hagar and their son, Ishmael, away from the family.

Yet Abraham's depth of loyalty and character is revealed when he rescues Lot from the kings who had kidnapped him, and when he intercedes for Sodom and Gomorrah. Finally, we see his common sense shining through when he settles a dispute that arose between his herdsmen and Lot's herdsmen. You see his desire to avoid conflict when he states, "Let's not have any quarreling between you and me."

You might also like to study about Ruth, another Steady Relator whose life is chronicled in the Bible. Here's the scenario: Her husband has recently died. Her mother-in-law, Naomi, also is a recent widow who is about to return to Israel. In their farewell scene, Ruth's friendship with Naomi tenderly invades our heart when she pledges, "Where you go, I will go; where you stay, I will stay;. . .where you die, I will die."

In her new country, Israel, Ruth can't wait to serve her mother-in-law. She goes into the fields to glean what has been left for the poor. She humbles herself for a friend. Can anyone forget the words of witnesses who sum up our high "S" Ruth? "Your daughter-in-law, who loves you, is better to you than seven sons." Thank God for our "S" mates. (The fascinating story of Ruth and Naomi is found in the Book of Ruth.)

THE COMMUNICATION STYLE OF THE STEADY RELATOR

Let's switch gears again and take a look at the communication style of the Steady Relator. High "S's" prefer an environment that is favorable, personal, and agreeable. They will make an effort to "set the stage" for communication, especially when that communication is of an intimate or romantic nature. A Steady Relator needs to see that you have a genuine interest in him or her as a person, and that what he or she is communicating to you has value and carries weight.

The high "S" may ask "how" type questions to gain clarification or reassurance. "S's" operate from a base of trust. As a result, they may be tentative in sharing their goals, aspirations, or deeper feelings until the proper level of rapport is established.

The high "S" will process information slowly. Anything regarding change must be presented in a positive and nonthreatening manner, followed by sufficient time to process the information, weigh its impact, and make adjustments. The high "S" needs reassurance about his or her role in any plans being presented. "S's" want their feelings to be considered as a part of the planning process. They need to know specifically what they are to do, how they are to do it, and the outcome that can be expected.

In order for Steve to communicate his deep and committed feelings to Susan, the setting had to feel safe to him. Susan could have helped her husband with reassurances that she is committed to him for a lifetime, and is genuinely interested in him both as a person and as her husband. Since it was a risk for him to talk, she needed to reassure him that what he had to say was valuable and that it wouldn't be casually dismissed.

What appears to be procrastination or inactivity in a Steady Relator may in reality be an attempt to gain the proper time to reflect upon the information that has been communicated to him or her. It is imperative, however, that the "S" communicates to his or her spouse that time is being spent in contemplation, and not merely in the avoidance of conflict.

WHEN COMMUNICATING WITH THE STEADY RELATOR, TRY TO AVOID...

- **Being pushy, overly aggressive or demanding.** All of these approaches make the "S" person feel threatened. Communication and intimacy can be negatively impacted when an assertive posture is used.

- **Being confrontational.** If you want to have intimacy with a high "S" person, the last thing you want to do is become argumentative or critical in your approach.

- **Being impatient or rushed.** Remember, "S's" need time to process information and to adjust. If you push for responses and answers, they feel threatened. This may cause them to become even more determined to withdraw.

- **Threats involving dramatic changes.** Your "S's" greatest fear is loss of security. Threats may paralyze him or her into inaction.

- **Making accusations.** "S's" become very defensive when their deep sense of responsibility is insulted, or their hard work is taken lightly.

WHAT TO SAY TO "S'S"

Want to open new doors to better communication with a high "S?" Here are some helpful lines and word pictures they will love...

- "You have such an empathy for people. It's almost like when I get cut, you bleed."
- "You are a cautious person. I've noticed how you study things before you get involved. It makes me trust your judgment."
- "I wish I had as much intuition as you do. It's like a sixth sense or something."
- "I love you for your kindness. You seem to always go the extra mile for people, even when I don't think they deserve it."
- "I feel like I can talk to you about anything because you always listen. Your interest in me makes me feel incredibly close to you."
- "I wish more people were as dependable as you are. I can always count on you."
- "I admire your consistency and faithfulness."
- "You always plan ahead. I know there won't be any surprises if you can help it."
- "You are so calm. Being with you is like taking a tranquilizer."
- "If there were more people with your compassion, this world would be a kinder place to live."

STEADY RELATORS AS LOVERS

Above all else, Steve and other Steady Relators are looking for evidence of security in their relationships. Trust and commitment, high on the list of components for satisfying sexual functioning, are foundational to them. Their approach to sex is emotionally oriented, constant, and sometimes reserved.

While "S's" are passionate, the setting and mood for lovemaking are important elements of their total sexual experience. Long-term relationships enhance sex for Steady Relators, but they have to be careful not to allow them to become boring and routine.

"S's" are open to intimacy in a favorable setting, but will withdraw affection and intimacy in an environment they perceive as unfriendly or antagonistic. While they are also people-oriented, the high "S" tends to be more introverted and less filled with optimism than the Influencer. "S's" are also much more passive in their approach to life. Steady Relators are not easily changed; they like to keep what is theirs. If yours is a more active personality style, and you want to develop intimacy with your high "S," you may have to do the changing.

THE NEEDS OF THE STEADY RELATOR

The high "S" puts a great deal of energy into trusting and being trustworthy. These are foundational qualities to building lasting intimacy in a relationship. While important to all other styles, too, trust is critical to the Steady Relator. If trust is ever violated once it has been established, it's doubtful that you will ever regain the depth of relationship you once had with an "S." They may forgive you, but they won't forget.

The high "S" person needs sincere appreciation for what he or she has done. Steady relators, more than any other style, tend to tie their self-esteem to the things they have done for you. Everything "S's" do is somehow connected emotionally to their relationship with others. For example, the female Steady Relator may dislike doing laundry. Yet she enjoys providing this service for the people she cares most about, her husband and children. In the same sense, she may not feel like having sex, yet more than any other personality type, she will comply for the sake of the relationship.

The male high "S," because of his masculine desire to be physically needed, will endeavor to set aside time to be with his wife and children. On the other hand, the high "S" male can be so "laid back" that it can drive the more active-style wife to frustration.

Steady Relators need repeated patterns in their daily lives. No, they are not in a rut, at least they don't see it that way. Predictability and a lack of change provide security, which is their primary goal. If there is going to be a change, they need time to adjust. The high "S" does not like surprises unless they are carefully planned in advance. Steady Relators need to have clearly defined expectations and parameters of responsibility, *especially* involving intimacy in a sexual relationship. Most of all, they need love, acceptance, and intimate contact that they can rely upon, no matter what.

SOME BLIND SPOTS OF THE STEADY RELATOR

Other personality styles may view the high "S" person as a spectator, noting that he or she never seems to really get involved. This can be especially frustrating to the more active styles if they are expecting the "S" to initiate intimacy or lovemaking. For this reason, it might be good for the "S" to take a little risk and be the initiator on occasion.

Because of their greatest fear, the high "S" will avoid situations or conditions that are perceived to be a threat to their security. In fact, they may become passively aggressive by "digging in their heels." This can cause them to appear to be stubborn or iron-willed. They may say "Yes" and give in, but they really mean "NO." Furthermore, while it may not be their intent, the high "S" can appear to be judgmental. "How many times have I told you…"; "I told you this would happen…"; "Why bother; you never listen to me anyway."

Steady Relators put a lot of energy into keeping things safe and secure for themselves and for those they care about. They avoid conflict and make peace, often by appearing to be self-sacrificing in the process. They may seem to enjoy being a martyr, but they don't see themselves that way. They often employ guilt as a method of gaining control. Because they focus on feelings, their desire is to motivate others with feelings.

If you want to point out a blind spot to a Steady Relator, it must be done without threatening his or her security in any way. Be sure you address the behavior rather than the person. Offering your "S" an alternative positive behavior to replace his or her blind spot is a crucial tactic. Any change you request requires them to step outside their comfort zone.

"S's" don't respond well to orders or tactics which make them feel inferior. If you are trying to badger your "S" into doing something, it simply won't work. Instead, a great question to pose to them is, "How would you feel about this, if it were happening to you?"

HOW THE STEADY RELATOR IS TEMPTED

No one is immune to temptation. However, because of the strengths and attributes of their style, Steady Relators are perhaps the most difficult persons to tempt. They are loyal to their loved ones, sometimes to their own detriment.

If we closely examine their reasons for intimacy, we can find some potential for temptation. "S's" are looking for a feeling of oneness with their partner, and intimacy and sex are part of the process of achieving that goal. When "S's" find themselves in a situation where they feel threatened or insecure, they may seek solace and security elsewhere in their quest for oneness. Steady Relators will endure a lack of intimacy, perhaps longer than the other styles, but, should they lose hope in the relationship, they may seek a change. Once this has happened, it is virtually impossible to get them back.

The male Steady Relator may succumb to temptation from a source close to him in friendship or in the workplace. He will respond to women who seem to provide the respect, admiration, sincere praise, and trust that he craves. If he is married to a more active-style person who continually applies pressure in some way, he may opt for the path of least resistance.

The female Steady Relator may succumb to temptation when she feels emotionally needed. Once she feels her relationship at home is lost, she may move on. Steady Relators are most vulnerable when they feel insecure, have lost hope in the relationship, and no longer feel a sense of intimacy with their mate. Only then would someone else, offering solace and a sense of oneness no longer found at home, be appealing.

Temptation for a Steady Relator, whether male or female, is most likely to be with someone he or she has had contact with in a close, intimate setting over a prolonged period of time.

THE STEADY RELATOR'S VIEWPOINTS ON SEX

Setting the male ego aside for a moment, it is fair to say, in general, that the high "S" view of sex is focused on genuine love and affection. These are people who are highly emotionally oriented, yet their approach is steady, calculating, and reserved. This is not to say they are not passionate. On the contrary, they are very passionate indeed. They are simply more concerned with the creation of the proper environment for love and affection prior to lovemaking than they are with having sex.

Romance and intimacy for both the male and female high "S" are important factors. Based on their gender needs, they may approach these aspects differently, but overall they are both seeking the security that comes from long-term relationships built on trust and filled with intimacy. For this reason, "S's" tend to have the most potential for a successful relationship with another Steady Relator or with a Conscientious Thinker style.

HINTS FOR HELPING THE STEADY RELATOR RELATE TO ANOTHER STEADY RELATOR

The Steady Relator will probably perceive another high "S" as dependable, self-controlled, patient, kind, accommodating, and attentive, thus promoting intimacy. Love and affection will be mutual and reciprocal. They will be supportive of each other but because they are slow to move or decide, little experimentation or change will occur over the years. It is more likely that a predictable pattern will develop, and boredom could result. Two "S's" will avoid confrontation and will seldom disagree openly or hurt each other's feelings.

In a nutshell—*For one high "S" to relate to another, they need to move at a steady pace, express sincere appreciation when deserved, and devote necessary time and effort to building a friendship from which intimacy will result. Each should strive to accept the responsibility for satisfying and keeping alive intimacy and sexual fulfillment for the other. If you are an "S," force yourself to ask questions about improvement, even if you are afraid of the answers.*

HINTS FOR HELPING THE STEADY RELATOR RELATE TO THE DOMINANT DIRECTOR

The high "D" is the greatest challenge to intimacy for the Steady Relator. "S's" are often intimidated by the high "D's" confrontational approach and demand for sexual activity. Because the high "S" tends to internalize feelings, he or she may not get angry, but may get even passive-aggressively: "I have a headache…"; "I'm too tired…"; "I had a bad day…"; "I don't feel well…"; "You always want…"; "The kids might hear…".

The Steady Relator will instinctively want to slow down the pace of the high "D," or to withdraw from the situation. The high "S" tends to perceive the Dominant Director as aggressive and unfeeling or too rough and physically demanding in his or her approach. However, there are some effective techniques that the high "S" can use to help overcome these perceptions.

One of the best things "S's" can do is to draw upon the "D" factors within their own personalities and use them to approach the high "D." In communication with the "D," the Steady Relator needs to be direct, to the point, and as specific as possible without getting bogged down in detail.

An "S's" interaction with a "D" might look something like the scene in *The Wizard of Oz*, when the Tin Man (a high "S" if there ever was one) tries to speak to the Wizard. As it turns out, the Wizard wasn't the terrible monster he attempted to make people believe he was. In fact, he turned out to be a mild-mannered and somewhat timid little man. The dreadful Wizard did not really exist at all.

The same is true of the high "D." When approached in a direct, no-nonsense, straightforward manner, that "D" can stand for Docile. A very successful Dominant Director was once heard to say, "Nobody realizes how much 'D's' need love."

In a nutshell—*When expressing your desires concerning intimacy to a "D," be brief, direct, and to the point. Don't ramble, repeat yourself, focus on problems, or make statements without support, like "You always..." or "You don't care...." or "You never...." The high "D" wants to be your best friend and lover. They desire to know what you want, and not a reinforcement of their failures or a story about your feelings.*

HINTS FOR HELPING THE STEADY RELATOR RELATE TO THE INFLUENCER

Intimacy with the high "I" should be a snap for the high "S." The Influencer likes to talk and, for the most part, the high "S" likes to listen. In fact, when it comes to intimacy, these two can be a great team. The high "S" enjoys listening to the high "I" talk about his or her needs and desires and will perform to be accommodating. On the other hand, the "I" seeks approval from the "S," and will attempt to perform accordingly.

There are, however, a few problems to overcome. For example, the Influencer craves change, excitement, and variety; they are impulsive, spur-of-the-moment people. Our Steady Relator, on the other hand, doesn't care for change, and seeks a slower pace. The high "I" wife may want to rearrange the furniture once a week. This drives the high "S" husband crazy. The Influencer husband may want to experiment sexually. This can make the Steady Relator wife a bit nervous. In an atmosphere of love, respect, open communication, and commitment, the "S" spouse is far more likely to adjust to the "I's" creativity.

The Steady Relator may perceive the Influencer as a bit egotistical, superficial, overly optimistic, glib, too self-assured, and inattentive. If this is your reaction, slip into the "I's" shoes for a moment. If you are an "S," and you're trying to understand an "I," think about how you would feel if you wanted people to like and accept you, but no matter how hard you worked at it, you never seemed to achieve your goal of feeling loved. That need drives the Influencer.

In some cases, that "I" can stand for Insecure, which causes Influencers to overuse their strengths. When dealing with the more inactive styles, such as the "S," "I's" may work harder at trying to get a favorable reaction. How would that make you feel? When dealing with the Influencer, don't forget to wear your "I" glasses.

In a nutshell—*To achieve intimacy, be friendly, responsive, and more talkative. This is easy for the high "S," because they are people-oriented. Be complimentary, letting them know what they did to make you feel good. Listen to the ideas and feelings they are expressing and support them in being intimate.*

HINTS FOR HELPING THE STEADY RELATOR RELATE TO THE CONSCIENTIOUS THINKER

The high "C" may be perceived by the Steady Relator as evasive, defensive, too focused on details, too cautious, and too compliant. There are, however, many similarities in the "S" and "C" styles. For example, both tend to be less openly intimate, less hurried, and somewhat passive in nature, and they are both reluctant to take quick actions without knowing what the response will be. The Steady Relator may perceive the "coolness" of the Conscientious Thinker to be personal rejection. As a result, the "S" may withdraw from what seems like an unfavorable environment.

Conscientious Thinkers require latitude and independence which the "S" may interpret as lack of interest. Much like the high "S," "C's" long for reassurance, precise expectations, and clearly defined parameters of intimacy and sexuality. The difference is, the "S" wants it personally communicated while the "C" may want to read about it. "C's" like to have their sexual roles defined but not imposed upon them. A "C" may become overly cautious and conservative in the process if he or she comes to believe his or her partner isn't satisfied. Conscientious Thinkers, like Steady Relators, may postpone intimacy if they perceive a risk.

The "S" and "C" styles can be very compatible in an intimate relationship since they are both passive and slow-paced. They have the capacity to give each other a great deal of time and care.

In a nutshell—*Be sure, especially when dealing with issues of intimacy, to discuss your ideas and recommendations for intimacy with a "C" in a calm, noncritical manner. Give them time to share their plans and thoughts for increasing intimacy. Be patient, persistent, and diplomatic while providing explanations to them. If they have difficulty verbally communicating, written correspondence may be the best option for both of you.*

PERSONAL AREAS OF GROWTH FOR THE STEADY RELATOR

After reviewing the various attributes of the Steady Relator, you may be interested in taking some new steps toward personal growth. If so, here are some practical suggestions for you to think about.

- **Try to be more open to change.** Change, in today's world, is the only thing that is constant.

- **Develop more flexibility.** Things do not always go the way we plan or according to schedule. As Charles Stanley said in a sermon he preached in 1994, "What happens to us is not as important as how we react to what happens to us." Flexibility is the key.

- **Increase your pace to accomplish your goals.** I'm not suggesting that you "throw caution to the wind." By all means, wear your seat belt, just go a little faster.

- **Work at expressing your thoughts, opinions and feelings.** This may require giant steps outside your "comfort zone," but you will not regret taking those steps.

- **Deal with confrontation constructively**. The Chinese character for "crisis" is a combination of the characters representing "danger" and "opportunity." Confrontation allows us to deal with issues we have kept suppressed. Confrontation may feel like you've entered the danger zone, but seize the crisis as an opportunity to clear the air, to share your ideas and feelings, and to learn.

- **Practice making decisions.** Learn to say "no." Prioritize your time investments and activities. No one else should take responsibility for your life. Don't allow a more assertive personality type to nudge you out of the driver's seat.

CHAPTER

The Cons
Thin

Cindy threw her book
into the kitchen. Bef
clipped a candy box o
pleated papers and the last of t
Dutifully, Cindy picked up the mes
lining up the remaining chocolates

It wasn't like her to hurl bo
worked for a large accounting firm,
apartment, was normally quite cont
few minutes later, she instinctivel
but her mind was speeding. "That
herself as she pulled into her com
again reading another romantic n
resemblance to real life sex!"

With that outburst, she felt en
lem seemed to be resolved, at least
it wasn't. By the time she left w

solutio
head or

Cin
with C
her ima
numbe
romant

Cin
figures,
satisfyi
a swee
Possess
convinc

Cir
uncom
"I enjoy
was at
enough
too mu

Wh
affectio
both w
sex. Bu

; to her sexual difficulties were careening around in her ce again.

ly had been married a little over a year, and her sex life uck had not lived up to the promises of either books or gination. Being an analytical type, she had purchased a of "how to" sex manuals. Lately, she had resorted to : novels. Neither approach had helped.

ly's superior planning, detail-oriented charts, graphs, and plus her persistence, had failed to unlock the secrets of a g love life. She didn't blame her husband, Chuck. He was and compliant man, much more laid back than she. ng a kind of "practice makes perfect" mentality, he was d that things would eventually work out.

ly was deeply committed to her marriage and felt rtable leaving such an important thing as sex to chance. d tonight," Chuck would say. "On a scale of one to ten, it east a six." Cindy would fume. A "six" was not good They were young and healthy: a "nine" or "ten" was not h to expect.

t Chuck did mind was Cindy's tendency to hold back . He enjoyed her touch, and just sitting by her while they re reading made him feel close to her and more ready for when Cindy started obsessing about sex not being a

"10," she would pull away emotionally and physically, making it hard to feel intimate.

Chuck wasn't always comfortable with Cindy's after-sex quarterbacking either. As soon as they were finished making love, she wanted to process and "deal" with what did or didn't go right. Chuck simply wanted to smile at her and go to sleep.

UNDERSTANDING THE CONSCIENTIOUS THINKER

Both male and female high "C's" have a tendency to take things a bit too seriously, including themselves. In relationships, they may dwell on things like, "He didn't kiss me good-bye." "She smiled at everyone but me." "Why doesn't he call when he's going to be late?" "She should know by now that I like starch in my shirts." These statements reflect difficulties common to any couple. To the high "C," however, they are taken personally.

"C's" bring a measure of perfection and stability to society because the Conscientious Thinker's greatest fear is criticism, confrontation, or changes in relationships.

When it comes to matters of the body and soul, Conscientious Thinkers are inclined to dwell on negatives, or what they perceive as negatives. They move cautiously and systematically toward intimacy. Their approach is designed to reduce any unfavorable response from their partner, and they typically want to think things through before making any moves.

"C's" try to anticipate any possible thing that could go wrong. As a result, they are the least spontaneous of all the styles. They may put things off, not because they are procrastinating but because they are not quite prepared. They tend to be the most introverted of all the styles, and generally have a soft-spoken manner. Here are some other helpful clues for recognizing high "C's..."

1. They lean toward perfectionism and seek to comply with their own lofty set of performance standards.
2. High "C" people are sensitive; their feelings are hurt very easily.
3. They fear criticism, confrontation, and/or changes in circumstances or conditions.
4. They strive to be accurate.
5. They want to know all the background information and details about everything.
6. The Conscientious Thinker needs clear explanations, and asks many questions to clarify instructions or issues. He or she is controlled, analytical, compliant, competent, and talented.

The strengths and weaknesses of the **High "C," Conscientious Thinker**, are listed on the chart on the adjacent page. As you know by now, any strength overused has the potential to become a weakness.

High "C"—Conscientious Thinker
chart of strengths and weaknesses

Strengths (General)	Weaknesses (General)
Analytical and idealistic	Moody and negative
Perfectionist and conscientious	Critical
Loyal	Rigid and legalistic
Self-sacrificing	Revengeful
Self-disciplined	Persecution prone
Serious and purposeful	Unsociable
Genius prone	Theoretical and impractical
Talented and creative	Has false humility
Artistic or musically gifted	Has selective hearing
Philosophical and poetic	Introspective, with low self-esteem
Appreciates beauty	Tends toward hypochondria

Strengths (Spouse and Family)	Weaknesses (Spouse and Family)
Sets high standards	Has unrealistic goals
Wants everything done right	Is too meticulous
Sacrifices own will	Lives through others
Encourages scholarship and talent	Is socially insecure
Content to stay in background	Holds back affection
Avoids drawing attention to self	Is antagonistic and vengeful
Is schedule-oriented	Is not people-oriented
Perfectionist, high standards	Is depressed over imperfection
Is detail-oriented	Chooses difficult work
Persistent and thorough	Is hesitant to start projects
Is orderly and organized	Spends too much time planning
Sees the problem	Self-deprecating
Finds creative solutions	Hard to please
Needs to finish what's started	Sets unrealistic standards

This chart was adapted from the Person to Person Certification Course by Sanford Kulkin, published by the Institute for Motivational Living, Inc.

THE CONSCIENTIOUS THINKER IN THE SCRIPTURES

Moses, one of the most prominent figures in the Bible, was a classic Conscientious Thinker. You probably remember that God went about getting our high "C" friend's attention with a burning bush. A "D" might have said to someone nearby, "Check it out." An "I" would have said, "What a fantastic sight!"—and then he would have moved on, hardly slackening his pace to make this observation. But what was Moses's reaction to the burning bush? He says, "I will go over and see this strange sight—why the bush does not burn up" (Exodus 3:3). "Why? Why? Why?" asks the curious "C," satisfying his or her desire for details and analysis.

Here's another fact about high "C's"—they tend to be content to stay in the background, out of the line of fire. Does Moses want to be a spokesman for God? Not on your life! "What if they won't believe me, or listen to me?" (Exodus 4:1). Fear of criticism or confrontation? You bet.

But remember Moses's attention to details in recording God's instructions about all the laws and the details for building the Tabernacle. Only a "C" could have written the Book of Leviticus! And only a "C" would have the patience to lead the children of Israel for forty years in the wilderness without going anywhere.

Mary, the mother of Jesus, also characterized our "C" personality style. Her encounter with an angel of the Lord sparks her analytical mind: "What kind of greeting is this?" And when told she will soon bear a child, she wants to know, "How could this be?" (Luke 1:26-34).

After Jesus is born, Mary considers all that has happened, mulls them over and over again, and appears to keep what she is thinking to herself: "Mary treasured up all these things and pondered them in her heart" (Luke 2:19). Mary (along with most Conscientious Thinkers) was a private, introspective person who apparently shared her thoughts sparingly with others, despite being the mother of the Savior of mankind!

THE COMMUNICATION STYLE OF THE CONSCIENTIOUS THINKER

Like Mary and Moses, Conscientious Thinkers as a group rarely could be characterized as "gabby." Their communication is carefully calculated and measured. The high "C" supports ideas and statements with accurate data—a lot of data—expounding on all the details of a situation to eliminate surprises. When they agree with you, they will be specific about what they are in agreement with. They fear criticism, however, and when they disagree they may be somewhat critical.

The Conscientious Thinker is patient, persistent, and diplomatic when providing explanations. "C's" have a tendency to "tell it like it is," but they are generally respectful of feelings in the process. They present things in a systematic and comprehensive manner. They seldom become emotional in the presentation of facts.

Much like the high "S," the "C" requires time to process and weigh information. In a confrontational situation, they will most likely become silent and attempt to withdraw. Given sufficient time, however, a "C" will carefully consider the controversy at hand and respond with the correct answer.

WHEN COMMUNICATING WITH THE CONSCIENTIOUS THINKER, IT IS WISE TO...

- **Offer as many details as possible.** "C's" value facts and guidelines. Phrases like, "I'm not sure, but…", "I don't know why, I just feel like it's a good idea…", and "That's close enough for me!" can be quite unsettling to the high "C."

- **Answer questions as specifically as possible.** Don't be vague or casual in your responses to the high "C." This is especially true when emotional issues, or matters of the heart, are being discussed.

- **Don't criticize.** High "C's" have a tendency to tie feelings of self-esteem to what they have done. If you criticize something your "C" has done for you, he or she may see it as a personal attack.

- **Don't generalize.** Making statements like, "You always do that…" will cause a "C" not to take what comes next seriously. In the "C's" mind, the word "always" is inaccurate and, therefore, your facts are wrong.

- **Don't react negatively.** A heavy sigh or roll of the eye in response to something a "C" may have said can hit him or her right in the heart, resulting in overly cautious behavior and extreme conservatism.

- **Give them time, but provide a deadline for decisions.** "C's" can get bogged down in details, often to the extent that they postpone decisions. If they perceive a risk to be involved, they can get caught up in the "paralysis of analysis." At times they may even decide not to decide.

On the other hand, an ability to carefully analyze things makes the high "C" an effective troubleshooter. If you need an objective opinion on something, ask a "C."

WHAT TO SAY TO A CONSCIENTIOUS THINKER

If you wish to touch the heart, body, and soul of a high "C," here are some word pictures and opening lines that may help...

- "You'll never know how much I love your thoughtfulness and the care you put into our relationship. You try so hard to make things better and better."

- "I can always count on you to have the most sensible, objective point of view. I don't know what I'd do without you."

- "I find your curiosity about things exciting and stimulating."
- "Thank you for not being impulsive when you're making a decision. I really appreciate the way you think things through."
- "I know that whenever I want something done right, I can count on you."
- "Until I met you, I didn't really understand what 'still waters run deep' meant."
- "When I need to figure out something, I can't wait to talk it over with you first."
- "Your attention to detail is invaluable."
- "You're a wonderful listener. You pay close attention to what I say and how I feel about things. I love that."

CONSCIENTIOUS THINKERS AS LOVERS

When Cindy talked to Chuck about sex at the start of this chapter, she was patient, persistent, diplomatic, and always to the point. "Chuck, I'm disappointed with what happened in bed tonight. I know it is not all your fault or mine. I love you dearly and I am convinced things can be better."

Like other Conscientious Thinkers, Cindy is straightforward and unemotional in presenting the facts. "As you know, I've read and done everything I know to do. I'm wondering how you would feel about us visiting a counselor who specializes in sexual difficulties...I would like to go." The "C's" solutions are well-researched and thought out.

When confronted, however, Cindy's natural tendency is to withdraw and become silent. Fortunately for Cindy, Chuck is supportive and patient. A Conscientious Thinker can be wounded deeply by disapproval, and perceived negatives can make him or her feel guilty and moody. If Cindy felt Chuck didn't care and she had tried everything, she would be prone to losing hope and becoming depressed. Since Conscientious Thinkers frequently measure their self-worth on performance, when things don't go well it is easy for them to develop a low self-image.

It would be easy for a Conscientious Thinker to become so focused on the technical aspects of sex that the sheer physical expression of good lovemaking is overlooked. In sexual counseling this is called "spectatoring," and is a major problem, particularly among men who suffer from fears about their performance. On the other hand, when in balance, the Conscientious Thinker's attention to detail and desire to be a good lover can work positively toward a healthy, joyful sex life.

NEEDS OF THE CONSCIENTIOUS THINKER

High "C's" need to see follow-through on commitments made to them. "C's" collect and analyze information throughout the day, and weigh it against the performance standard they have set for their partner. For example, if a spouse forgets to keep a promise, a "C" might view this as a failure of their partner's commitment. The "C" may feel rejected or unimportant because what he or she expected to happen, didn't. This could trigger a withdrawal of affection or intimacy.

Conscientious Thinkers move slowly and tentatively. They need time and space to process romance and to be assured that there are no ulterior motives involved. Since they are prone to be easily hurt, it is important for their partner to keep a record of positive experiences relative to the relationship, intimacy, and sex. Carefully, using caution and a nonthreatening manner, draw "C's" out in order to clarify their expectations.

The high "C" also stands for compliant. "C's" will comply with their partner's desires and wants if they are within the standards they respect. The high "C" person is an incredibly warm and loving person under the right set of circumstances.

High "C" people have a lot of cookbooks, actually read instructions, plan shopping trips, and generally schedule every aspect of their lives. Of all the styles, they seek a design for intimacy the most. They need to know what is expected of them.

"C's" are creative people, as well. For example, high "C's" make good musicians because they practice over and over and over. They may get frustrated, however, with the high "I" personality who plays by ear. The high "C" practices endlessly, while the

Influencer just sits down and creates. In the music of intimacy, while the "I" may be more spontaneous, the "C" will keep trying until he or she gets it right.

SOME BLIND SPOTS OF THE CONSCIENTIOUS THINKER

Being cautious and conservative can become compulsive behavior when carried too far in a relationship. The time spent by the high "C" processing information may be seen by some other styles as procrastination, laziness, lethargy, or simply "dragging their feet." Many a high "C" has been labeled as an "underachiever," when in fact, he or she was simply taking time to make things correct.

Conscientious Thinkers may inhibit intimacy by looking for negatives, then feeling guilty or becoming moody. They may become overly critical of themselves or their partner, see no hope and become depressed. Their critical thinking often revolves around themselves, causing them to become introspective and self-centered.

For the male high "C," being a good father, a good husband, and a good lover is imperative. However, he will set a very high standard for these things on himself, perhaps even one that he himself cannot live up to.

The high "C's" standards for his or her spouse can be unrealistic, too. A statement was made by an Influencer wife about her high "C" husband: "I have never done anything that was quite good enough. There was always something he tried to correct about me." The female high "C" naturally tends to seek emotional fulfillment through performance, rather than expecting and receiving unconditional love or acceptance.

To make matters worse, the Conscientious Thinker woman often has the perfect romantic scenario in her mind and each time it is not met, she suffers a bit of disappointment. This may cause her self-esteem to erode because a standard she has set was not met. She might have a tendency to absorb the negatives in her relationship as personal failures. This can cause her to eventually pull away from all intimacy.

Because their feelings of self-worth are based on performance, "C's" often have blind spots. When pointing out a limitation to a high "C," it is extremely helpful to use the PAR—Problem, Action, Result—format we suggested earlier (see chapter 4 under the heading, "Blind Spots of the Dominant Director"). However, for the high "C" person, you'll want to de-emphasize the problem, recognize all the things the "C" has done right in the past, and suggest an alternative positive behavior. This will go a long way toward helping a "C" spouse overcome a blind spot without endangering the quality of intimacy you have already established together.

HOW THE CONSCIENTIOUS THINKER IS TEMPTED

Because of their aversion to risk-taking and their high standards, high "C's" are not easily tempted or distracted. The Conscientious Thinker has to be involved in situations that "make sense." What they are doing and who they are doing it with needs to feel right, add up, and meet their standards. If a door to temptation can be opened, it usually results from their tendency to be "conditional" in terms of their emotional support and affection. The high "C" female may use affection or sex as a tool to obtain her needed loyalty and support. The high "C" male, on the other hand, expects to be trusted as a result of proven trustworthiness. They will both be drawn to people who meet these needs.

Conscientious Thinkers may adopt a "show me" or "wait and see" posture in terms of a relationship. They are attracted to people and situations that provide them with a controlled environment and meet their standards. In both work tasks and interpersonal relationships, two high "C's" can be very compatible. Temptation may sneak up on them, because they are so focused on what they are doing that they don't see it coming.

The door to temptation can also be opened by a spouse who is overly critical of the high "C." As they withdraw affection from the critic, they might well seek another outlet for that affection. They may focus on people they know (friends or co-workers) who appear to be safer, and more understanding of their needs.

Cindy's high standards kept her searching for the best within her marriage. Her temperament was not one that includes a lot of risk-taking, trying to find a magical "perfect lover." Her choices were clearly defined and had to feel right. Only her own unrealistic expectations could make her vulnerable to someone else.

THE CONSCIENTIOUS THINKER'S VIEWPOINTS ON SEX

High "C's" approach their sex life in much the same way they do most other activities—striving for correctness. The male high "C" may be concerned about his physical performance. In fact, there can be an actual dialogue during lovemaking, consisting of clarifications and questions relating to performance.

For the female high "C," because of their intense emotional needs, sex must have clearly defined parameters. Conscientious Thinkers tend to be conditional in terms of their expressions of love or affection. Therefore, sex can be used as a reward for good performance in another area, or withdrawn as a punishment for poor performance.

High "C's" are self-sacrificing, serious, and purposeful in their approach to lovemaking. While they enjoy sex, they may not enjoy it simply at face value. The woman may see the sex act as a symbolic gesture exemplifying the union created by the respect, trust, and loyalty she has given to her husband. The man may see the process building up to the sex act itself as a task to be completed to achieve a goal. Because he tends to be process-oriented, his performance in the pre-coital stages of lovemaking is on an equal plane with the sex act itself. Basically, because they are perfectionists, high "C's" may be the best lovers, especially in a "technical" sense. One thing for sure, they enjoy practicing until they get it right!

HINTS FOR HELPING THE CONSCIENTIOUS THINKER RELATE TO ANOTHER HIGH "C"

One high "C" may view another Conscientious Thinker as a perfectionist who is accurate, thorough, systematic, agreeable, and adaptable. As a result, the two of them can live and share intimacy together. They will cooperate, devise careful plans, and create extensive control systems in lovemaking and intimacy. Their concern for the quality in the relationship will override their individual needs. They may even compete to see who can be the most correct in meeting the needs of the other.

In a nutshell—*Two high "C's" will build a relationship by being persistent and moving at a slow pace. They can discuss the facts and details of their intimacy with each other. They will strive to remove any apparent threats or flaws in the relationship. They are well prepared and compile information to help them plan things carefully. They will be accepting and encouraging of one another because they recognize the need for these things in each other.*

HINTS FOR HELPING THE CONSCIENTIOUS THINKER RELATE TO THE DOMINANT DIRECTOR

A real challenge to intimacy with the high "D" is the high "C's" perception that "D's" are argumentative, dictatorial, haphazard in their approach to problem-solving, arrogant, domineering, nervous, pushy, and impetuous. The high "C" may attempt to remedy these perceptions through the use of external authority, such as books, tapes, taking them to seminars or to church, and so on, in order to deflect the perceived demands of the high "D." The goal of the high "C" in all of this is to make the "D" comply.

The high "C" may become defensive when the high "D" is pushing for results which nullify intimacy in the "C's" mind. High "C's" may not verbalize their feelings, however they may be thinking something like, "He just doesn't understand. I wish he would just leave me alone." There is a potential for major tension between these two styles. The high "D" is focused on the forest while the high "C" is studying the trees. Both may eventually retreat out of frustration.

In approaching intimacy with the high "D," Conscientious Thinkers need to speak simply and directly. For example, if a high "D" husband says to his high "C" wife, "How was your day?" she may be inclined to give him every detail of her experiences during the day. That's not what he's looking for. His real question is: "Was your day good or bad?"

Make verbal interactions with the high "D" short and to the point. They like questions to which they can respond with either "yes" or "no." With some practice, given the high "C's" gift for creativity, most questions can be phrased to elicit this type of response.

In a nutshell—*To improve intimacy, be more direct and brief, even though it is a stretch for your personality. Limit details and options but share what you like in a clear, straightforward and concise manner. Don't be discouraged by the "D's" tendency to take the lead. Let him or her lead you where you want to go, and try not to become defensive if things don't go your way. The "D" won't notice if things aren't perfect.*

HINTS FOR HELPING THE CONSCIENTIOUS THINKER RELATE TO THE INFLUENCER

Dealing with the Influencer may present the greatest relational challenge to the high "C." The Influencer is seen by the Conscientious Thinker as being egotistical, superficial, overly optimistic, glib, too self-assured, and inattentive. On the other hand, Influencers may find their enthusiasm dampened by the pessimistic attitude of the high "C."

Conscientious Thinkers tend to highlight possible dangers and problems. For example, the high "I" wife comes home from work excited about an upcoming business trip to Southern California. Her high "C" husband immediately begins to quote recent statistics on airline crashes, the high crime rates in Los Angeles, and earthquakes. She is thinking Disneyland, he is thinking disaster!

In a nutshell—*To build intimacy with your Influencer, be friendly and complimentary. Make every attempt to catch his or her enthusiasm and reflect it back. Listen to your "I's" ideas and recognize his or her efforts to please you. Allow "I's" to talk themselves into where you want to go by being positive and not critical. Try not to "rain on their parade" until they have had some time to tell you about how great it will be.*

HINTS FOR HELPING THE CONSCIENTIOUS THINKER RELATE TO THE STEADY RELATOR

Intimacy will be affected if the high "C" critically views the high "S" as impassive, apathetic, too accepting, lenient, possessive, complacent, or nonchalant. The fact is, a high "C" wants the very relationship that the "S" can provide. Since the high "S" has loyalty and is family-oriented, he or she will want to please the "C" in every way.

In a "C"-"S" relationship, the Conscientious Thinker may be his or her own worst enemy. For this reason, "C's" should focus on the positive traits of the "S" and the relational things held in common. Viewing these in a positive light will help eliminate perception differences and improve the environment for intimacy.

For example, the high "C" agrees with the Steady Relator on the importance of cooperation, reducing risk, and using caution in making decisions. The high "C" may be concerned, however, that the high "S" may not be precise enough in their approach to solving a problem, or dealing with a situation. In addition, the high "C" may cut short, or ignore altogether, the need that the high "S" has to develop a relationship. These are cautions that should be addressed.

In a nutshell—*For the sake of intimacy, the high "C" needs to be amiable and relaxed in his or her approach to the high "S." Take some time and work at establishing a friendship that is warm and personable. Show your "S" sincere appreciation for things done well and encouragement for those that need improvement.*

PERSONAL AREAS OF GROWTH FOR THE CONSCIENTIOUS THINKER

If you're a high "C," by now you're wondering exactly what you can do to improve yourself and your relationship. Here are a few possibilities you'll want to think about.

- **Concentrate on doing the right things in addition to doing things right.** Make a task of developing more intimacy with your spouse by openly sharing your feelings with him or her. It may present something of a risk for you; however, the rewards are great.

- **Be less critical of your spouse's ideas and methods.** For example, he or she may prefer not to take the same road from home to a vacation destination as you do. Take some time to study the other route, and consider its positives. It may be more interesting. Your lover wants to feel good about himself or herself, so deposit praise in their emotional bank and reap intimacy dividends.

- **Be more decisive.** Force yourself to make decisions with limited information from time to time. The most important decision you can make is to increase your positive self-talk. "Life is not perfect, but life with my partner is the best, and God gave me the perfect partner for me."

- **Focus less on facts and more on people.** It may not hurt to relax your standards a bit when it comes to what you expect from others. Try finding the things that are right about what they do, rather than being critical of them. In addition, don't be so hard on yourself.

- **Take a risk from time to time.** Our old friend the turtle has much to teach us in this regard. The only way he makes forward progress is by sticking his neck out! You may miss your "window of opportunity" by waiting for conditions to be just right. Be more spontaneous in your lovemaking and intimacy. Try something new and exciting.

- **Develop thicker skin**. Make a decision to not let things bother you, or to let your feelings be hurt too easily. Check some of the baggage you are carrying about past hurts; it may be time to let go and give it to God.

CHAPTER EIGHT

The Gender Gap

"Ouch!" Jim yelped, limping into the kitchen. "Who left Barbie in the hall?" He held the flaxen beauty by one of her perpetually pointed pinkies. Jim's daughter, Tiffany, gasped and rescued her precious treasure mid-air.

"Is she all right? I forgot—"

"Next time, Tiffany," Jim barked, cutting her off, "keep her off the floor!" Tiffany scurried out of the room, inspecting Barbie for any evidence of damage.

"You're in a fine mood this morning," Jim's wife, Karen, remarked. She was already dressed and ready to leave for her teaching job. Sometimes Jim hated her morning chipperness—especially *this* morning. He pulled up a chair and plopped down—making it clear that his ire went beyond the hallway encounter with Ms. Plastic Perfection.

"As a matter of fact, I am pretty steamed." Jim continued, "I thought we were going to have some 'fun' last night and it didn't happen. I wish you would let me know beforehand if sex is the last thing on your mind."

"You expected to have sex last night?" his wife asked incredulously. She joined him at the breakfast table but made no move to eat. "Jim, you know the last three days have been absolutely crazy for me. I'm swamped at work, Mother has required hours of my time, and I had a paper due for the graduate class I'm taking. Sex didn't quite make the top ten list. I never even thought about it."

"Now *that's* a true statement..." Jim said curtly. His voice rising, he added, "I'm always at the bottom of your list! You had plenty of time to talk to your friend Annie on the phone...."

Hearing Jim's sarcastic tone, Karen was tempted to get up and storm out of the room. But it wasn't like her to leave things unresolved between them. Instead of leaving, she poured them both a cup of coffee and sat back down. "Jim, I'm sorry. I didn't know you were planning on our making love last night. You should have said something. I have a lot on my mind but I could have been persuaded. I talked to Annie because she listens to me when I want to tell somebody my troubles. When I try to do that with you, you act like Mr. Fix-it, and then get mad if I don't do what you tell me."

"It doesn't make a lot of sense to talk about problems if you don't want solutions, Karen," Jim added in an exasperated tone. "Besides, that's not really the issue. I have a lot going on in my life too—you know I'm up for a promotion. Sex helps me relax."

"The whole household knows you are under stress right now, Jim." Tears began to well up in Karen's eyes. "To be honest, when you're this grouchy, I don't feel good about making love to you."

"Well, if you *would* make love, I'd be more relaxed. And I'd feel more like being nicer to you," Jim snapped.

Karen jumped to her feet. "I shouldn't have to have sex with you for you to be nice to me."

"It isn't as simple as that, Karen," Jim replied.

And indeed it isn't.

MORE THAN PERSONALITY DIFFERENCES

Jim, a "D," and Karen, an "I," have to adjust to differences in their personalities in order to communicate well. But they also have to remember that, simply because they are male and female, they look at life through different glasses. The basic design of men and women provides each with a way of viewing the world that is neither right nor wrong, better or worse, than the other sex—it is simply different.

Obviously, physical differences (including brain organization, reproductive capacity, and musculature) affect and influence emotional and thinking capabilities. The individualized but sexually distinctive perspectives men and women hold, when taken together, provide the only holistic view of the truth.

In other words, Jim and Karen both have a point.

"MALE AND FEMALE, HE CREATED THEM"

When Karen was born, she was welcomed into a world of pink. People lowered their voices when they talked to her and commented on her dainty hands and beautiful nose. People touched and cuddled her far more than they did her future spouse. Jim was dressed in blue and was bounced around and told how tough he was. When he fell, he was brushed off and sent on his way.

By the time Karen and Jim were toddlers, Jim had learned to use the drawers in the kitchen cabinet as a ladder to climb up to the cookie jar or to look at life from a higher perspective. His greater musculature and high-power chemistry resulted in his getting into trouble on a fairly regular basis. When Karen wanted a cookie, she would charm a passing adult to give her one, or to lift her up so she could see life from on high. Karen and Jim both craved cookies and a new view of life, but they had different ways of getting what they wanted.

Before they entered preschool, they knew there were two sexes in the world and that Karen was like the "moms": Mommy, most teachers, and baby-sitters. Jim wasn't. Armed with such truth, and the reality that he was probably never going to behave in a fashion those "moms" would like, Jim began to work on his independence. Dad seemed to approve, and Jim gradually realized that growing up involved breaking away from the women in your life and becoming your own young man.

There was no such crisis or conflict for Karen. She identified with the "moms" and grew up wanting to feel close to and accepted by them. There was no pressing reason to distinguish herself from the people who cuddled, loved, and took care of her. Her sense of who she was did not have to come about by building defenses and rebelling. She could be comfortable seeing herself as being in sync with others, rather than being different from them.

GENDER ACROSS THE YEARS

In school, Jim liked to play outside in groups, sometimes with leaders who established or maintained rules. He and his other male friends liked to tell stories and joke with one another. The most important among them gave the orders and got the other boys to follow. Meanwhile, Karen played in small groups. She and her friends didn't joke so much or tell stories on each other. They liked feeling connected and close. No one was too obvious about wanting to be the "boss" either. Instead, all the girls longed for a best friend.

By the time they began dating in college, Karen and Jim lived in different worlds, each with its own set of rules and language. Jim's world was a hierarchical one. Great vigilance was required to maintain his due position. Life's challenge was to protect himself from being put down, and conversation was a tool used to help maintain the upper hand. Life was a struggle and his goal was to preserve his independence and avoid failure.

Karen was more concerned with maintaining social and emotional connections. For her, life's task was to preserve intimacy and avoid isolation. Conversation helped her confirm, support, and reach consensus in order to avoid being left out or rejected.

Just as when they were toddlers, both Karen and Jim had the same goal—they wanted to be in relationships with others. Their focus on how that might be accomplished had always been different.

- Her focus was intimacy achieved through closeness and connection.
- His focus was on independence achieved through power and accomplishment.

Because of these fundamental differences, Jim and Karen measured successful relationships by separate standards.

RELATIONSHIPS, BUT HOW?

Not long after they started dating, Jim announced he had agreed to go overseas for a semester. He explained to Karen that the opportunity would have lifelong repercussions for future employment. While Karen was happy for Jim and wanted him to go, she was furious that he had not consulted her before making the decision. If she was as important to him as Jim said she was, she couldn't fathom why he had not asked her before he obligated himself.

Did Jim see it the same way? Of course not. To Jim, asking Karen what to do would have made him feel like a child forced to get permission. Status is measured in a man's world by making decisions and giving orders.

- Her desire to be consulted did not mean she wanted to manipulate, make demands, or keep Jim from doing what he wanted. She simply needed evidence that he was committed to her and that she was part of his decision-making.
- His desire was to improve his earning potential. He wanted to demonstrate that he was capable of taking care of her.

Bad as they felt, neither Karen nor Jim understood that they had not rejected one another—or their relationship.

CHOOSING THE RIGHT LOVE POTION

Well, Jim and Karen got past that obstacle, and now they are married. Today they still find themselves tripping over classic male/female stumbling blocks.

- She wants him to be warmer to her before she feels comfortable making love. She is longing to feel connected to him in a way that translates into her language of closeness and intimacy.

- He wants assurance of his prowess as a lover and then he will feel close. Once he feels close, he will be warmer toward her.

When Jim says, "Give me sex first, then I'll be nicer to you," he is saying, "Your willingness to have sex with me affirms me as worthy to be your lover. It validates the appropriateness of my physical desire. I need to assure myself I am independent and acceptable. Once I'm reassured, I can risk being intimate."

Melting into the arms of a woman may feel wonderful, but it conflicts with a lifetime of effort directed toward vigilant assertiveness. It also conflicts with his drive to convince the world that he is separate and different from his mother—from all women. Becoming as unlike mother as possible means rejecting characteristics associated with women, such as compassion, sensitivity, and expressing emotion.

Most men grow up denying, or at least ignoring, their inner thoughts, wishes, fears, and needs. After finding his value through performance, the deep sanction of a loving sexual act provides a man with a refuge for unconditional acceptance. One has to wonder if this isn't why men sometimes approach sex with such fervor—for many it is the only place a man can feel completely safe to be emotionally intimate. Being vulnerable is limited to late hours, after sex, and the dark. The potential for conflict here is quite evident:

- The more a man views himself as "in charge" of his wife, the more he will consider sexual rejection as a denial of his dominance over his wife. He may feel compelled and justified to demand sex.
- Women are not likely to respond, literally or figuratively, to displays of power. For them, connectedness is the love potion they can relate to, and it is what turns them on.

Karen and Jim's dilemma can also be considered from another standpoint—the different way men and women use their brains to solve problems. A man will typically see the details of a situation, while a woman will grasp the overall picture. The distinction can be illustrated by considering the different illumination of a flashlight and a floodlight. While both shed light, the flashlight pinpoints details in a specific area, whereas a floodlight illuminates an entire area.

Jim's flashlight was on: "Why aren't we having sex?"

Karen's floodlight was on: "What's wrong with our relationship?"

"AS IT WAS IN THE BEGINNING..."

Lest you are tempted to dismiss all this as modern-day pop psychology, the basic struggle between a woman's desire for intimacy and a man's quest for independence and status is clearly identified by the events of the Garden of Eden. God's plan was for a world in harmony. Man and woman were designed before the Fall to be intentionally different and complementary. There was meaning and purpose in the very fact that there were two sexes. Their differences helped them define what it meant to be a male or a female.

Yet men and women were also made in the image of God, and God is a God of relationship. He sent His Son to ensure we would be in everlasting relationship with Him. God's image is reflected in humanity through the cooperative partnership of men and women.

"Woman is not independent of man,
nor is man independent of woman."
(1 Corinthians 11:11, NIV)

Indeed, man was not "good" until there was woman. The lives of men and women were to be bound up with one another. They were to marry, procreate, and together have dominion over all of creation (Genesis 1: 26-27).

The woman was declared a "helper" that was fit for the man (Genesis 2:18). Nowhere in the Bible do we find the word "helper" used to imply inferiority. In fact, God Himself is described as a helper, ministering to His people.

Before the Fall there was no secret, shame, or divisiveness—male and female natures blended to complete one another. That the woman was taken from man reflected their unity, and the fact that both owed their life to God. No animal was made as they were. Only one conclusion can be possible in looking at the original plan—the two sexes were to be bound together in a cooperative partnership.

Cooperation became difficult, impossible some might say, when the female abused her rights to co-dominion over the earth by eating what she was told not to eat. The male, whose desire had been to be in unity with the female, found harmony with his wife impossibly challenged after he placed it above harmony with God. Active participation and passive compliance were equally condemned. Adam and Eve were forced out of the Garden—out of harmony—and found themselves no longer interdependent in healthy and gratifying ways. Their shame triggered blaming and efforts to shift responsibility.

HER DESIRE FOR HER HUSBAND

But what happened next provided the foundation for Karen and Jim's (and all other opposite-sex couples) relationship difficulties. God brought certain consequences to bear upon his first couple. A woman's pain in childbearing would be multiplied—a pain that experience tells us extends beyond birth (Genesis 3:16). Her caretaking responsibilities have the potential of leaving her exhausted and too distracted to focus on lovemaking.

But more significantly, the woman is told that, henceforth, her desire would be for her husband but that he would rule over her (Genesis 3:16). Simply stated, she would want one thing and her husband would want another—there would be conflict.

While men might like to interpret desire for her husband to mean women will greatly desire them sexually, it appears not to be the case. One of the major frustrations expressed by men against women is that women appear to be ambivalent about sex. They accuse women of avoidance or at least inertia when it comes to freely expressing sexual pleasure.

Others suggest that the passage means that women want to control men. The women's movement is cited as proof that a woman's real desire is to take over the man's rightful position or at least be in direct competition with him. Such a conclusion is based on the belief that there has been a perversion of the basic nature of women as a result of the Fall, and that women reject who they really are.

Research and experience don't support such a theory. While some misguided females might think something is to be gained by rejecting the nature of their sex, preferring to think and act like men, most women continue to focus on relationships and connection with others as their major concern. They don't adopt the male emphasis on superiority, status, and highlighting of differences and distinctions between people. Curiously, even those women and men who are apt to be most vocal in supporting equality of the sexes are now involved in weekends where they seek to get in touch with their respective "goddess" or "warrior" within.

WOMEN WHO LONG FOR INTIMACY

What was really changed by the Fall? At the heart of the struggle between the sexes is the woman's unreciprocated longing for intimacy with a man. She wants to be heard and understood for what she says, and she wants communication to be a two-way street. In other words, her man should understand her, but she wants to understand him as well. She can only do that if he reveals to her the full dimension of who he is. Intimacy needs are so high for some women that they outweigh consideration of their own well-being. To that end, ponder the book titles available:

Sweet Suffering: Woman as Victim
Why Do I think I'm Nothing Without a Man
Men who Hate Women and the Women Who Love Them
Women Who Love Too Much

For the male, the Fall meant he would find himself in conflict with his helpmate. His task in the world would therefore be more burdensome, because he could no longer count on her full support. The world man faced would be one in which his labor would be hard and never-ending.

Instead of harmony with humankind, the earth, and God, life outside the Garden meant surviving in a hostile environment. To endure, performance would become critical and competition with others would be routine. Increasingly, man would be defined by his work, not by his relationships—with women or with God.

Whether we attribute the difficulties between sexes as a breech in the original design defaced in the Garden, or explain it away as socialization or mere biological differences, the challenge remains the same: How do men and women strike a balance between two basic needs?

She needs intimacy.
He needs independence.

HIS NEEDS/HER NEEDS: MALE/FEMALE PERSPECTIVES

Charts, by necessity, eliminate the nuances and exceptions of their subjects, but they also simplify and help us hone in on pertinent details. What follows is a synopsis of how differences between the genders are likely to be experienced in real life.

WHAT WORKS IN THE BEDROOM?

Men are not inherently evil because they are visually aroused and think about sex more than women. They were designed to respond in a way that makes sex a priority. This does not imply that it is their first priority, but it does suggest a man's sexuality is

GENDER NEEDS		
	THE MAN'S PERSPECTIVE	THE WOMAN'S PERSPECTIVE
Men and women have different needs.	Requires respect, independence, admiration, trust, to be physically needed, and to have maleness affirmed	Requires understanding, affection, love, romance, honesty, being emotionally needed, communication, security, time and attention
Men and women are stimulated sexually in different ways.	Aroused by visual Aroused by responsiveness of partner External focus	Aroused by touch Aroused by intimacy: words, actions, and attitude of partner Internal focus
Men and women have different sexual responses.	Often initiates sex Quick arousal Not easily distracted	Less frequently initiates Slower arousal Can be distracted from sexual arousal at most any stage
Men and women experience orgasm differently.	Can reach orgasm quickly Capable of one orgasm Recovery time needed for additional response Prefers orgasm for satisfaction	Slower to reach orgasm Capable of multiple orgasms No recovery time needed for additional response Emotional orientation tolerates sex without orgasm
Men and women have different sexual fears.	Performance, partner rejection, impotence, intimacy	Partner indifference, being unappealing, a physical focus that excludes emotionality and/or romance
Men and women have a different focus.	Seeks relational fulfillment through physical satisfaction Has a segmented or compartmentalized view of life: home, family, work, social, church, etc. Listens defensively with self-interest foremost Prizes independence Sees world as hierarchal Communication used to ensure status Uses affection to get sex Sex has high priority	Seeks relational fulfillment through intimacy Prefers secure environment with harmony and balance "Listens" emotionally for degree of closeness Prizes connectedness Sees world as relational Communication used to negotiate closeness Uses sex to get affection Sex is not prioritized

CHART 8.1

going to be important to him. It untangles why he can love his wife and still have intrusive sexual thoughts about other women. It explains why men so easily sexualize ordinary events or comments.

Studies in brain hemisphericity reveal that a man's brain processes visual information differently than does a woman's. Her brain is more sensitive to the emotional content of stimuli; the muse who noted, "It's all in the wiring," was right! With such differences in biology and socialization, it should be no surprise that we process romantic and sexual information differently. For example, pornography is almost universally purchased by men, while women often bury their noses in romantic novels.

When sex is meaningful to them, women can be responsive and creative in the bedroom. But research consistently reveals that men push for a "rougher," more experimental sex life. A quick encounter will probably not leave a man unhappy. A woman might be very unhappy indeed afterward, unless his passion somehow conveyed that her lover was completely enamored with her.

A touch of impulsiveness and more initiation by the female pleases most men. In fact, men desire more from their partner sexually than women do, who opt for love and intimacy over technique. It's quite possible that a man and woman's sexual encounter will be perceived in very different ways. He excitedly believes she is turned on by his technique; she assumes his passion is fueled by his deep feelings for her. Lost in the romance and erotica, the end result is an experience that transforms two into one.

HOW GENDER AFFECTS OUR PERSONALITIES

The importance of this chapter is to help you see that despite the significant impact of our individual personalities, gender provides an even larger bias that effects the expression of our basic traits. Whether a person is a "D," "I," "S," or "C," he or she will function within those parameters as a male or female. Consider the information on chart 8.2 on the following two pages.

Just how does this chart translate into real life? Remember Don, our male Dominant Director? His personality need to be in control feeds into his masculine need to ensure he is in a "one-up" position. Lovemaking and most everything else Don does is directed toward his craving to affirm that he is important. His wife's positive response in bed would prove that she found him attractive, manly, and skilled. If she wasn't responsive, he would convince himself that her needs were minimal and that since he is in charge, fulfilling his needs should be sufficient for her as well.

PERSONALITY DATA/GENDER NEEDS COMPARISON CHART

Greatest Fear	Resulting Evironmental View	Demonstrated Behavioral Style	Male Needs and the Style Employed to Meet Them	Female Needs and the Style Employed to Meet Them
"D" **Being Taken Advantage of**	Sees the Environment as... *Antagonistic or Unfavorable*	Dominant and direct Initiates action Impatient Confrontational Decisive Strong-willed Independent	Expects *Respect* for who he is Seeks to gain *Admiration* and appreciation via accomplishment Demands to be *Physically Needed* Must have his *Ego Built Up* by achievement and winning Gains *Trust* by verbalizing, "Trust Me!"	Desires *Affection* on demand Expects *Understanding* "Tells it like it is..." to gain *Honesty* Desires to be *Emotionally Needed* as a result of giving or doing for others Derives *Security* through independence Demands *Time* and *Attention*
"I" **Loss of Social Approval (Rejection)**	Sees the Environment as... *Positive, Friendly, or Favorable*	Influencing People-oriented Optimistic Active and positive Enthusiastic Demonstrative Disorganized	Wins over or influences others to gain their *Respect* Likes verbal *Admiration* Desires to be *Physically Needed* by being demonstrative Wants to have his *Ego Built Up* by verbal praise, sometimes solicited Builds *Trust* through communication and flattery	Seeks *Affection* through verbal expression Makes clarifying statements and asks questions to gain *Understanding*; wants to talk Demonstrates *Honesty* in sincerity of verbal expression Wants you to become an "open book" to be *Emotionally Needed* *Security* is obtained by talking things out and receiving a verbal reassurance Wants you to spend *Time* listening and to pay *Attention* when they talk to you

"S" **Loss of Security and a Change in the Status Quo**	Sees the Environment as... *Favorable but Tentative*	Stable and steady Quiet Sympathetic Peacemaker Loyal Possessive Resists change	Gains *Respect* through consistent performance over time which leads to... *Admiration* from those closest to him Desires to be *Physically Needed* by nurturing and relationship Wants to have his *Ego Built Up* by sincere appreciation and honest praise Builds *Trust* over time in close relationships	Gives *Affection* to get affection Displays empathy to others to gain their *Understanding* of her Demands *Honesty* in a passive-aggressive manner Involves herself with others to be *Emotionally Needed* Will become self-sacrificing to attain *Security.* "A bird in a cage is secure; not free, but secure." May withdraw affection to obtain *Time* and *Attention*
"C" **Criticism or a Change in Circumstances**	Sees the Environment as... *Unfavorable Due to Antagonistic Factors*	Compliant Sensitive Analytical Perfectionist Conscientious Pessimistic Introverted	Gains *Respect* through demonstrated competence Prefers *Admiration* for ideas or methods employed in task completion Desires to be *Physically Needed* as an integral part of a larger entity; i.e., family, relationship Wants to have his *Ego Built Up* by doing things right and being recognized for correctness, loyalty, faithfulness, competence, etc. Expects *Trust* because of demonstrated trustworthiness	Expects *Affection* in return for being supportive and loyal Will explain position with supportive facts and data to gain *Understanding.* "This is how I feel and why I feel that way." Demonstrates *Honesty* and cannot imagine why people would not be honest in return Strives to be *Emotionally Needed* by complying with acceptable parameters Builds *Security* by calculating outcomes and employing a more cautious approach Schedules *Time* and focuses *Attention* by removing distractions, normally involving a task

MALE AND FEMALE "D"

A very high-scoring Dominant Director male would have difficulty with intimacy because it would require a level of vulnerability he would find too risky. The fear of being taken advantage of—of not getting his due—would keep him from sharing his most intimate needs.

A female Dominant Director might express her feminine perspective in several ways. The bottom line is, she would want to be in charge. She would likely have very definite ideas as to how the sex act should go but she may or may not be openly directive. She might use seduction and sexual enticement to get her way. One could expect that some female Dominant Directors might adopt behavior that is somewhat exhibitionist in an effort to ensure an impact, and give her an edge.

MALE AND FEMALE "I"

The Influencer's basic need to communicate and enthusiastically relate to others is a very natural role for a woman. She wants to connect, and that requires knowing as much as possible about her partner. Like our example, Isabella, her natural openness to life in general and her desire to please may make her more comfortable with sexual experimentation than women of other personality types.

A male Influencer wants to talk as well, but the conversation might be slanted more toward assurance that he is measuring up well as a lover. He would probably be creative in his sexual approach because approval is important to him. Pleasing his partner enables him to avoid rejection in an area that is highly linked to his sense of masculinity; therefore, sex is a high priority. His preference would be for his partner to demonstrate her response to him in active ways, both verbally and physically.

MALE AND FEMALE "S"

While we know men worry about performance, the male Steady Relator worries that not measuring up will disrupt his world. He may suspect or know something is wrong but be extremely reluctant to rock the boat to find out, or to try to make things better.

Steve, our example of a Steady Relator, and others like him, might drop into a routine that, while not bad, becomes something of a rut in its safety. Bringing up need for more creativity may trigger his own or his partner's dissatisfaction, and require change. Since he doesn't want to take risks with the status quo, changes are likely to be incorporated gradually.

The female Steady Relator would also need to feel very secure about her relationship before she would suggest changes that might disrupt it. First of all, she is biologically less sexually aggressive than her man. Second, she has been socialized to let the male lead. Considering those factors, it might be difficult for her to initiate sex or be sexually forward, unless she was sure this pleased her mate.

Dissatisfaction with her sex life might be expressed in passive-aggressive ways, such as seeming willing to go along sexually and then not responding. It is also plausible that a female Steady Relator may sublimate unmet sexual desires through other activities such a childrearing, volunteerism, or making a very open and hospitable home.

MALE AND FEMALE "C"

Male or female Conscientious Thinkers are going to approach sex with expectations of competence. They will try hard to please and desire acknowledgment of their efforts, in order to make love-making satisfying. Feedback needs to be specific and focus on demonstrated competence.

A female Conscientious Thinker, like our example, Cindy, especially appreciates verbal responses that let her know exactly what her partner finds pleasing. She expects honesty and wants to be able to share what and why she feels the way she does sexually. Her high expectations may make it hard for her to accept the vicissitudes of a normal sexual relationship. If things don't go well, she may claim too much of the responsibility.

The male Conscientious Thinker is burdened with desiring to do the right thing and feeling he must direct the show. He may become too distracted by technique to guarantee a mutually satisfying experience. In the extreme, "C's" could approach sex in a regimented, ritualistic, and rapid way.

Since he is sincere in his efforts to please, suggestions for "lightening up" or "going with the flow" may be taken as criticism, rather than efforts to enhance the romantic aspects of love-making. If he gets too discouraged and analytical, he could decide to avoid sex rather than struggle with the possibility that he's not measuring up. His worst fear would be to experience erectile difficulties due to performance anxiety.

Fortunately, no matter what their personality types may be, most husbands and wives share the same motivation—they want their relationship to be as meaningful as possible. Sometimes gender issues get in the way or give the appearance that men and women have impossibly different agendas. Personalities and sexual attitudes are shaped by gender, genes, role models, environments, relationships, learned values, spirituality, and many other variable factors. Yet in the end, the miracle is that men and women are more alike than different.

MOVING TOWARD MUTUALITY

Co-author Sandy once asked his wife, Patty, to define the male ego. She reflected for a moment and then responded with, "It's a picture the man has of what he should be."

Depending on his experiences and learning, "what he should be" can be a healthy male image worthy of striving for. Or it can be distortion of what it takes to be a real man. Too often the male ego is an impenetrable mask of masculinity behind which the real complexity of a man lies. It is a mask used to hide the true self.

Men of the nineties are rightly reluctant about revealing their true selves. Less than a generation ago, being a real man was less confusing but more emotionally restrictive. The women's movement focused on freeing men and women to be whomever they wanted to be. It was mistakenly believed that distinctions between the two sexes would dissolve.

For a time, everyone from researchers to fashion designers chose to ignore or discredit anything reflecting men's and women's innate sexuality. It was assumed that all women, given the chance, would want to become active in the paid working world, and that they would adopt the competitive, one-upmanship style of men to do it. Meanwhile, liberated men would support this feminine invasion. They would display greater willingness to bear the responsibility of home and children. The trade off for men would be that they could finally cry, show emotion, and be "Mr. Mom" if they wanted to—and women would love them more.

But the reality was different from the vision. Tender men who job-share turned out not to be the choice to whom most women made a lifetime commitment. Opportunities for women to work outside the home, while increasing (by the mid-nineties one half of medical and law school students are women), have not changed the focus of the woman who heads a major company.

Her priority continues to be the connection she feels with family and/or employees.

A man may cry at his daughter's dance recital, but his sense of protectiveness and desire to be strong and independent in order to take care of her materially and emotionally remains. The new order has not changed a newly learned old truth—social roles have little to do with a person's intrinsic masculinity or femininity.

We remain wedded to our basic natures. Men who are packed off for sensitivity training are being asked to talk and think more like women. Women who attend assertiveness training sessions are trying to adapt to the more aggressive style of men. There is no dispute that learning one another's viewpoint will help us to communicate better and will increase the odds of intimacy between us. But this does not mean that we must change innate styles or become someone we aren't. God clearly honors our gender differences and distinct approach to life, because He created us to complement, not duplicate, each other. Shouldn't we honor one another in the same way?

PUTTING IT ALL TOGETHER

In simplest terms, exaggerated by living in a fallen world, in their approach to life...

Man is more physical.

Woman is more relational.

A man may feel threatened if he is shown to be wrong or discounted. To feel masculine, he requires respect and approval.

A man's greatest vulnerability lies in threats to his masculinity and his sexual relationship.

A woman judges her life by her ability to be involved with others. To feel feminine, she requires connection and intimacy with her lover.

A woman's greatest vulnerability lies in feeling unloved and/or unlovable.

Getting along is not simply a matter of a husband or wife thinking, "I'm going to change who I am." It boils down to working with who and what each one of us already is. Unfortunately, while home is meant to be a haven where we are safest to be who we most authentically are, it is also the place where gender differences are most acute and stressing.

Here are some suggestions for declaring truce in the war between the sexes:

Work on establishing meaningful and intimate communication.

1. *Men and women are to be emotional counterparts to one another.* Men must stretch as much as possible to relate to women on an emotional level. Women do this well and can be a man's greatest resource in learning to express emotion.

2. *Increase understanding of the feeling level of communication by using "word pictures."* For example, a woman will catch the fresh-

ness, nuances, and power behind her husband's expression of love if he places his morning newspaper down and shares, "You know something, Sweetheart? My love for you is as new as this newspaper, every morning."

(The alternative, "I love you, Sweetheart," emanating from somewhere behind the paper, is better than nothing, by the way!)

3. *Watch out for compartmentalization.* Men particularly tend to view segments of their life as separate and independent. We are all designed to have our emotional, physical, and spiritual life integrated.

4. *Be honest.* There is no better way of getting what we want than by clearly spelling it out, then participating in conversations that explore ways to realize our desires. Be creative. If letter writing helps, do it. Pay attention to the times you feel safest in your relationship (sometimes after sex) and risk sharing then.

5. *Make your spouse a priority.* Spend quality time together when you can enjoy uninterrupted conversation. Show you value him or her by being sensitive to the differences in male/female communication style.

Work on building and reinforcing your spouse's self-image.

1. *Don't major on minors.* The very differences that looked so exciting while dating sometimes become major irritations after the wedding. Focus on reinforcing the good. You may find that

negative behavior disappears without having to say a word, if compliments are given when something is done right!

2. *Watch your body language.* Giving positive verbal feedback can be undermined if gestures and expressions signal that we are unsatisfied, angry, disgusted, or offended.

3. *Work at recognizing and removing your own masks.* Our families should be a place for experiencing unconditional love and acceptance. Be open to your husband's or wife's loving desire to help you be who you are.

4. *Honor your spouse with sincere efforts to know him or her.* Can you name your spouse's favorite activities? Preferred color? Who are his or her friends? How does he or she feel about his or her job and co-workers? What hopes and dreams does he or she have for the future? What fantasy would he or she like to see come true?

5. *Don't demand perfection.* You and your spouse are on the same team, and nobody's perfect.

6. *Encourage one another to have a positive attitude.* When it comes to positive attitudes, we could all take lessons from a young boy Sandy once overheard.

The boy was out in the yard throwing a baseball up in the air and trying to hit it with a bat. Before throwing the ball up each time, he said to himself, "This time, a home run."

As he threw the ball and swung, Sandy heard, "Oops! Strike one!"

The boy picked up the ball a second time, "Oops, Strike two!"

With a look of determination on his face that would rival any big leaguer, he threw the ball a third time. "Strike three. You're out!"

The boy stared at the ball lying in the grass at his feet and then threw the bat down. A smile suddenly exploded across his face, and Sandy heard him exclaim, "What a PITCHER!"

A positive attitude is essential as husbands and wives pass through the changes and challenges of a lifetime. There will be misunderstandings. There will be confusion and disappointment. There may even be times when all seems to be lost. But those two unique creations—male and female—were originally designed to fit together perfectly. Marriage is the one setting in which that unity—emotional, intellectual, spiritual, and sexual—can safely take place. And it is in the marriage bed where each partner has the matchless pleasure of saying, both in actions and in words, "In you, my love, I have finally found the other half of myself."

PART II

Counsel From the Heart of a Pastor

INTRODUCTION TO PART II

In the previous eight chapters you have been reading about sex and about how our sexual personalities can be blended together so that marital intimacy is enhanced. With this section of the book, we will alter course a bit. We will close the bedroom door and roam through the rest of the house—after all, a great marriage is more than great sex.

I invite you to let me share some things I've learned about a fulfilling marriage and have conveyed to hundreds of couples in my pastoral and seminar ministries. Although we can never forget our personality style, I want you to see that there are some general principles for marriage that apply to every style.

Sandy, Mary Ann, and I believe that what occurs in the bedroom is predetermined largely by interactions between you and your spouse which take place long before you enter the sacred chamber of your bedroom. So please read on, and let me open my heart to you as you work at developing the intimacy God wants you and your loved one to share.

—Duane Storey

CHAPTER NINE

Tending the Marriage Garden:

Developing Intimacy

A cool, gusty breeze from Oregon's Pacific Ocean kissed our faces as we walked along the beach enjoying a cloudless spring day. Wave after wave slapped at the sandy shore, showering us with mist. It was chilly, but warm feelings penetrated our cold bodies as we walked with arms around each other's waist. Over twenty-five years of marriage had passed.

"I love you, Marty, more than words can express," I told my wife quietly.

"I know, Duane," Marty said with a smile. "I feel the same about you."

Looking at her radiant face, I confessed, "Marty, during these last few weeks I've felt closer to you than ever before. You are not only my wife and lover, you're my best friend. I could never imagine life without you."

For a few moments, time stood still as I held her close to me, the wind tossing her hair while engulfing my face in its fragrance. Our marriage flashed before me, the good and the not so good. If there was one thing I knew about our marriage, it was that Marty and I had finally reached a wonderful, fulfilling level of intimacy.

PLANTING SEEDS OF INTIMACY

Our friend Allan Petersen says, "The seeds of marriage success are already in your marriage. You must water and fertilize them."[1]

Allan is so right. The God who created you has planned a garden in the form of your marriage—a garden that must be tended carefully. He has given you the responsibility to serve as a gardener: You plant the seeds, pull up the weeds, water and feed—and watch the intimacy grow and flourish.

What is intimacy? Webster defines it as "the state of warm friendship developing through long association," suggesting informal warmth or privacy of a very personal or private nature. I would be the first to say that the intimacy Marty and I now enjoy was not always there. In the early years of our marriage, I lived in my own world and would not let Marty into my life. We had to discover that intimacy does not flourish by accident; couples have to work at it. That was what Allan meant when he said you must water and fertilize the strengths you bring with you into marriage.

One of the most challenging areas in marriage is the difference in value systems. Couples come from two different families, have experienced different upbringings, possess different personality styles, and often grow up in different religious denominations. Differences in values frequently hinder couples' attempts at intimacy.

It's helpful to take the time to both list and talk about different values. As our relationship grew, Marty and I learned to recognize the various values that sometimes came between us. We examined them, studied the Word of God, came to agreement on some, and learned to accept others.

STEPS TOWARD AGREEMENT

Marty and I worked through this process for years. We asked God for guidelines. As we searched the Scriptures, we discovered Romans 4:13-18 (NIV):

> Therefore let us stop passing judgment on one another. Instead, make up your mind not to put any stumbling block or obstacle in your brother's way. As one who is in the Lord Jesus, I am fully convinced that no food is unclean in itself. But if anyone regards something as unclean, then for him it is unclean. If your brother is distressed because of what you eat, you are no longer acting in love. Do not by your eating destroy your

> brother for whom Christ died. Do not allow what you consider good to be spoken of as evil. For the kingdom of God is not a matter of eating and drinking, but of righteousness, peace and joy in the Holy Spirit, because anyone who serves Christ in this way is pleasing to God and approved by men.

The Amplified Bible states, "Let all men know and perceive and recognize your unselfishness—your consideration, your forbearing spirit" (Philippians 4:5).

Our pursuit also led us to Romans 15:3, "For Christ (gave no thought to His own interests) to please Himself; but, as it is written, the reproaches and abuses of those who reproached and abused you fell on Me" (Amplified Bible).

Faced with different values, and yet being determined to come to an agreement one way or another, here are some things Marty and I learned to do:

- Whatever the circumstances or issue, we got the subject out in the open.
- We shared our emotions concerning the conflict—anger, rejection, frustrations, etc.
- We acknowledged that our emotions were real. We didn't deny the other's right to feel the way they did. We encouraged each other to try to share emotions in positive ways.

- We tried to determine the source of our values.
- We studied God's Word and what it said about our values.
- We asked ourselves if there were any personal "right" we should yield, in order to demonstrate Christ-likeness.
- We developed a plan to change any behavior in question.

When a partner is willing to yield a behavior or change a value, trust is established. The more we trust, the better our communication. When communication is positive, closeness develops. Friendship is strengthened. And intimacy begins to grow.

DIFFERENCES IN SEXUAL VALUES

However, even when intimacy is alive and well, Christian couples sometimes have differing ideas about sexual behaviors and techniques, and those conflicts can cause stress in marriages. Some differences are minor—for example, married couples are frequently heard to complain that either the husband or the wife wants sex more frequently than his or her partner. Some argue that morning encounters make their day, while others are sure late night rendezvous are the only way to go. Disagreements like these are irritating, and create disharmony. But like the proverbial toothpaste-squeezing wars and toilet-lid skirmishes, good communication and a willingness to compromise usually results in a truce.

Resolving differences in sexual values can be considerably trickier. The sense of what is appropriate goes far beyond habit and cherished memories of how "mother" did things or wanted them done. The core belief attached to behavior that violates our value system sends off bells and whistles that can leave us guilt-ridden, immobilized, or angry. Most seriously, an individual may feel that he or she is in violation of God's standards. Men and women face conflict when the desires or demands of a spouse place them in what appears to be a no-win situation.

Anyone who teaches marital enrichment seminars knows that the most frequently asked "values" question couples ask is about oral sex. While younger married couples often include this behavior as part of their routine lovemaking, older couples in their late forties and up are far less apt to participate. Arguments over its appropriateness can occur in any age group, but are most often found among older couples.

Most objections to oral sex center over one partner's belief that God did not intend sexual desire to be expressed except through intercourse, which of course has the possibility of pregnancy. Oral sex's association with prostitution, homosexuality, and sex without commitment cause some to question its correctness. Most frequently, however, objections to oral sex are the result of a person of authority, sometimes a pastor, having instructed a man or woman that such behavior is abhorrent and displeasing to God.

Couples also find their values at odds over the use of birth control, the number of children they should have, and whether Sunday is or is not an appropriate day for sex. The purpose of this book is not to address all of these issues. Rather, it is to encourage you that the better your communication and understanding of one another, the greater the intimacy you will nourish between you; and the heightened level of intimacy generated will increase the odds that even these serious issues can be addressed and resolved.

Any morally sensitive person should be concerned with the misuse of sex in his or her home, as well as by our culture. The evidence mounts that disaster occurs when people reject standards meant to preserve their emotional and physical health. But this should never result in the conclusion that sex is bad, and that its expression should be severely restricted.

It's no mistake that God did not give humankind a sexual checklist for married couples. He speaks to us about sex through the passion of the Song of Songs. He created us to be "naked and unashamed," and instructed us to "leave" parents and "cleave" to our spouse. In other words, we are to grow up—and do all which that implies. We are to increase our self-awareness, make an effort to understand our partner and ourselves, and reach beyond ourselves to meet the desires and wishes of our spouse. Sex should bind us together with cords of love, not rip us apart.

THREE ELEMENTS OF ADAPTING

Nothing requires a flexible, cooperative attitude in marriage more than sexuality. We all benefit from flexibility, allowing ourselves to be molded into the space God has given each of us in our spouse's life. No matter what the issue we're facing, no matter what value we're trying to consider, being adaptable requires three essential elements:

- ***The Element of RISK.*** Every time you place yourself in the position of having your greatest fear realized, you are taking a risk. Once we face our fears and share our feelings, something wonderful begins to happen. We become a little more real emotionally, and our spouse is drawn closer to us.

- ***The Element of MEETING NEEDS.*** Examine the needs of your spouse's behavioral style. Observe his or her likes and dislikes. Ask if there are needs he or she feels are not being met. Usually men are not particularly discerning in the need-meeting area, and have to be told. Imitate Christ's attitude of being more interested in serving than being served.

- ***The Element of WIN/WIN.*** Most all of us believe in the win/win theory, but there are times when we seem to lose by giving in or giving up something. Is this really losing? Whenever we meet our mate's needs, we help the marriage succeed. When our spouse wins, we win, too, because we are one. Someone once said, "When I found out how to lose, I found out how to win." There is a lot of truth in these words.

A RETURN TO ROMANCE

Another factor in feeding and watering our marriage garden is the enhancement of romance. Allan Petersen has said there is no romance in marriage. What he means is that romance is in *people,* and people put romance into marriage.

One man took his wife on a dinner date. What's so unusual about that? For one thing, they both were dressed formally, so she was surprised to find herself on a back road headed into the mountains. The husband pulled onto a forest service road and stopped at a beautiful meadow with a gorgeous view of snow-capped mountains. He opened her door and escorted her to an elegant table covered with a white lace tablecloth, matching napkins and china, candles and silverware. Attending them was a tuxedo-clad waiter. This romantic husband had hired a caterer to give his wife of over twenty years a wonderful culinary experience in the mountains.

Is there any question whether this couple's romance carried on long into the night?

Another man sent a limousine to pick up his wife. The limo took her to a local airport where she was given a plane ride over the Cascade Mountains. When she landed at her destination, another limo took her to a restaurant where she met her husband for a wonderful dinner and night away from home—a night they would long remember.

All this might seem almost too extravagant, but the idea is to think about ways you can romance each other. Remember the enchanted evenings you spent together before you were married, before the kids and bills? Why not try to relive some of those moments again? Discover new ways to romance your spouse. At least every other week, why not make a date to be alone together?

You are the designer—design an atmosphere where both of you can fall in love again. Bring each other little gifts—they don't have to be expensive. If you can't afford a diamond, bring a favorite candy bar or a single rose. All these things build intimacy. And in marriage, romance is the icing on the cake of a deep, intimate friendship.

FIND GOOD SAME-SEX FRIENDS

Strange as it seems, intimacy is enhanced by a little distance now and then. In order to increase intimacy, couples need personal space, and this invariably happens when men and women develop other same-sex friendships.

In many marriages, the wife is the husband's best friend. Until the recent Christian men's movement in America, the prevalent attitude was that men are strong and do not need anyone but their spouses. Wives were supposed to draw strength from their husbands and, in turn, give their husbands all the emotional support necessary. This sounds neat and tidy, but life really doesn't work that way. Husbands and wives set each other up for failure by placing the responsibility to meet all their emotional needs on their partners.

When America was an agrarian society, there was plenty of time for women to be with women and men to be with men. Even in the business world, some males followed in their father's or uncle's footsteps. There was time for "man talk," because there was time to be together.

Today, in America's high-tech culture, families are often separated. Grandparents live in one place, parents in another, and children somewhere else. Emotional needs that were met by dwelling together and working together go unmet today, especially among men. The result is that millions of Americans will experience psychiatric illness during their lifetime, and a vast percentage of us will be in psychotherapy at some point.

Women need to release their husbands to other men, encouraging them to find male friends for accountability, companionship, and strength. Women, too, need to have female friends. Often a woman understands another woman in a way her husband simply cannot. By spending time with others, couples are refreshed and excited once they are reunited with their spouses. There are new things to talk about, new stories to tell, new ideas to share. The result will be newly revitalized intimacy.

INTIMACY AND PRAYER

There is another intimacy seed called *prayer*. The apostle Peter spoke of husband/wife relationships in his first epistle and shared the reason for developing a good relationship: *so that nothing will hinder your prayer*. I don't believe he was only writing about private prayer. He was writing about praying together.

Praying with their wives is one of the last things some men do. Why? Perhaps it is because prayer places them in a position of dependence upon God, and men like to be able to depend upon themselves. Maybe it's because they feel a sense of helplessness, and don't want to ask for help. Husbands may not want their wives to see them in a dependent situation. Yet my wife's testimony about our praying together is this: "I feel closer to you when we pray together, Duane, than at any other time. For me, praying together is the most intimate thing we do."

Kneeling beside the bed, holding hands, lifting up our praise and our requests, and entering into His presence may indeed be the most intimate thing any of us ever does with our spouse. It is part of God's design, because spiritual intimacy is another vital part of marriage. When a couple's body, soul, and spirit are in harmony with one another and with their Creator, physical intimacy becomes reminiscent of Paradise, and love returns to Eden.

OPPORTUNITIES FOR GROWTH

1. On a separate sheet of paper, list ten values that are important to you. Ask your spouse to do the same.

- Beside each value, number it **1** if it is *very important*, **2** if it is *quite important*, and **3** if it is *less important.*

- Compare your list with your spouse's, and circle those things which are most important to each of you. Discuss why they are.

- Put an **X** beside those items which you believe are not as important as the others. Discuss why this is true.

- Where there is disagreement about a particular value, discuss how this might cause you to differ in your decision-making regarding finances, child raising, lovemaking, and so on.

- Talk about ways you will deal with your values when you disagree with your partner.

2. Discuss how you will practice being adaptable to meeting your partner's needs.

3. Complete the sentence: *Before we were married, I liked it when you...*

Discuss your answers. Are you still doing the same thing(s)? Why or why not? Will you consider doing them again?

4. Complete the sentence: *I feel loved when you...*

Discuss why you feel loved when your partner behaves toward you in this way.

5. Complete and discuss the statement: *I feel romantic when you...*

6. At least once a week for the next four weeks, kneel and pray together before you go to bed. Discuss how you feel about this. (But do it anyway!)

CHAPTER 9 Endnote

1. J. Allan Petersen, *The Myth of the Greener Grass* (Wheaton, Illinois: Tyndale House Publishers, Inc., 1983), p. 178.

CHAPTER TEN

Do You Respect Me?

Communication is the bedrock of a healthy marriage. Understanding gender differences and personality styles is of tremendous value in building a strong union. And intimacy, based on trust, is indispensable for sexual harmony. But there are other elements that cannot be overlooked as body and soul are brought into unity. One essential element is mutual respect.

No matter how much talking we do, and no matter how much information we carry around in our heads, unless we hold our spouses in a place of the highest regard, our marriages will suffer. Are you respectful of your spouse? You may answer "yes" quickly, but are you demonstrating your respect consistently? Here are some guidelines about marital respect against which you may want to measure your marriage.

RESPECT IS DEMONSTRATED WHEN HONOR IS DISPLAYED

Do you remember the phrase in your wedding vows that declared, "to love, honor, and cherish?" Gary Smalley, in Love is a Decision, shares that "honor is the foundation for all healthy relationships."[1] Smalley states that the Greek word for honor carries with it the idea of great weight. When you made your wedding vows, you were declaring that your mate's opinion would carry a great deal of weight with you.

After the Persian Gulf War, Carl was contacted by a company who was hiring construction people to spend one year working in Kuwait. These workers would make over $90,000, and housing and food would be furnished. To take advantage of this offer, the hiring company was asking for several hundred dollars up front for processing applications, visas, and other documents.

Carl's wife, Marge, was uncomfortable when she heard about those up-front costs. She sensed something might be seriously wrong and cautioned her husband not to write a check without making a serious investigation of the company's business history.

Carl felt rushed. He had been told time was running out, and that most of the jobs had already been taken; only a few remained.

"Don't do it!" Marge said.

"But this is such a great opportunity for us," Carl insisted. "After a year, we'll be home, out of debt, and we'll be able to buy a new home. This is too good to pass up."

Carl wrote the check against Marge's better judgment. And guess what? The "great opportunity" was a scam.

Had Carl honored his wife? No, he placed no weight on her opinion, even though she told him on more than one occasion that she didn't feel any peace about the decision. Consequently, there was no peace, no harmony, in the decision. And there was less intimacy in the home.

When a man honors his wife, he hears and listens to her and does not criticize her opinions. Sarcasm is inappropriate, too. Consider your wife's personality type and her strengths. Where do her strengths undergird your weaknesses?

MEN REVEAL RESPECT WHEN THEY PRIZE THEIR WIVES

The apostle Peter, in his first epistle, instructs, "Husbands, in the same way be considerate as you live with your wives, and treat them with respect as the weaker partner" (1 Peter 3:7, NIV). The word "respect" in this passage means "to prize." One woman, speaking to a friend, humorously said, "My husband would loan me out before he'd loan out his car!" She thought he prized his car more than his marriage.

How should husbands prize their wives? Ephesians 5:28 indicates that husbands ought to love their wives as their own bodies. In verse 33, we read that the husband must love his wife as he loves himself. How do men love themselves?

- Most men don't treat themselves harshly. Prizing a wife means, rather than treating her harshly, she should be treated with tenderness, gentleness, and affection.
- Most men don't despise their weaknesses. If anything, their weaknesses are ignored or covered up. Wives don't need to have their weaknesses pointed out, either. Instead, wives need to be protected and loved unconditionally.
- All men want their needs met. Rather than demand that their own needs be met, husbands should seek to meet the needs of their wives.

As we've already seen, women treasure relationship and thrive on affection. A husband who cherishes his wife provides an incubator of nurture and growth.

WIVES HONOR THEIR HUSBANDS WHEN THEY DEMONSTRATE RESPECT

Ephesians 5:33 goes on to say, "And the wife must respect her husband." This passage reflects a male's need for respect from his female. Men innately crave the respect of their wives. Often I will hear a woman say she doesn't love her husband anymore. However, with a little counseling and practical guidance, love can be restored. But when I hear a woman say she doesn't respect her husband anymore, my heart nearly stops. Of all his needs, except for the need of knowing Jesus Christ as Savior, respect from a man's wife may be the greatest. Without it, he begins to die inside.

A man is to love his wife as Christ loved the Church. A woman is to respect her husband by deferring to him, and submitting to his headship. Both of these require an act of the will. Whenever a marriage begins, a new entity is formed where both husband and wife come out from under the control of their parents. The husband becomes head of the new family. The wife, rather than being controlled by her parents, yields to her husband.

However, in Ephesians 5, emphasis is not placed on authority and power. Emphasis is placed on accountability to God and sacrifice. In his book *God's New Society*, John Stott writes, "If 'headship' means power in any sense, then it is power to care, not to crush, power to serve, not to dominate, power to facilitate, not to frustrate or destroy."[2]

Men are not given power to be critical and to impose restrictions. A husband's God-given authority is meant to empower and to free his wife from rigidity. The apostle Peter inspires couples to help each other to become everything God wants them to be:

> Finally, all of you, live in harmony with one another; be sympathetic, love as brothers, be compassionate and humble. Do not repay evil with evil or insult with insult, but with blessing, because to this you were called so that

you may inherit a blessing. For, whoever would love life and see good days must keep his tongue from evil and his lips from deceitful speech. He must turn from evil and do good; he must seek peace and pursue it (1 Peter 8:11).

When a couple acknowledges Jesus Christ as Lord and seeks to obey Him, the result is honor and harmony in relationships. When His ways are ignored, dishonor and power struggles take place, and intimacy is unable to grow.

RESPECT IS REVEALED WHEN COURTESY IS PRACTICED

Common courtesy goes a long way toward practicing respect. Here are some practical ways of extending courtesy to your spouse:

- Helping your wife put on her coat
- Opening a door for your wife, allowing her to enter before you do
- Never belittling your spouse's opinions
- Never using demeaning words or name-calling
- Calling home when you're going to be late
- Helping with dinner
- Helping with the dishes after dinner

- Saying "Thank you," even for the little things he or she does
- Saying "What can I do to help?"
- Not being too busy to listen
- Giving full attention when he or she is talking

RESPECT IN YOUR SEX LIFE

As we've already learned, sex can be extremely gratifying or it can be disappointing. Gratifying sex occurs when a husband and wife enjoy communication, understanding, intimacy, and respect for each other. Here are some ways respect can be shown in your sexual relationship:

Understand that male/female sexual desires differ. This is an initial step in practicing respect. It bears repeating—males have a more direct approach to sex than women, while a woman's desire is to be held, touched, and kissed. Ann Landers once reported a study where over seventy-five thousand women stated that being held and touched would be satisfying to them without sexual intercourse. The implications of this are enormous. For most women, affection is needed for sexual intercourse to be satisfying.

"He only touches me and holds me when he wants something," has been echoed over and over in counseling offices. And husbands invariably respond, "She never wants to make love. She would be satisfied if we never had sex again." If this is an area of concern in your marriage, please read chapter eight again—together.

Don't use sex as a weapon. Women, more than men, withhold sex in response to other concerns. When a husband has disappointed or wounded his wife, she may feel uninterested or even distressed at the thought of being sexually intimate with him. Sometimes, even without consciously meaning to, she "punishes" him by rejecting intercourse. If a woman is hurt, she may not be emotionally able to respond to her husband's touch. If she is angry, she may not allow herself to enjoy sexual intimacy.

Men have their own way of using sex as a weapon. When a man feels rejected, he may operate in lust rather than in love. Love values the partner; lust sees the partner as an object to fulfill an intense, driving urge.

If a man shuts his wife out emotionally, personal gratification dominates the marriage bed and the total relationship ceases to be the focus. The problem with lust is that it dehumanizes. Sometimes lust in marriage is so subtle that couples cannot pinpoint what is wrong in their sexual relations. They just know something is not quite right.

In both scenarios, the spouses feel used, and the use of sexual "weaponry" should send a warning flag that something else is wrong. When couples begin to communicate about their sex lives, the issues that surface can be dealt with and intimacy can be restored. If after communicating about sex things do not improve, couples should contact a godly counselor or a doctor.

Consider your partner's feelings. There are times when your spouse may not be ready for sex. A woman's need for lovemaking can fluctuate, and men may also have varying degrees of sexual desire, especially when they are involved in highly demanding jobs. The Scriptures do state our bodies are not our own. Some people think spouses should never deny each other sexually unless illness occurs. However, when legitimate reasons such as illness exist for postponing sex, it should not be viewed as rejection. The male ego will probably feel rebuffed. But when intimacy already exists, postponing sex for a few days doesn't need to have a negative impact.

Respect for your spouse, taking into consideration gender, personality style, and unique individuality, are vital to intimacy in marriage. Once you've developed respect, you'll discover that some wonderful other qualities are awaiting you—joy, acceptance, and encouragement. You'll be building an affair-proof marriage.

OPPORTUNITIES FOR GROWTH

1. Do this exercise together. Take two sheets of paper. Working separately, list all the ways you currently show respect for your mate. Go through your list and after each statement, number it 1, 2, or 3 (3 = Very Important; 2 = Moderately Important; 1 = Not So Important).

When you finish, share your statements and add anything you've left out. *Before* each statement, place the number your partner gave it.

SAMPLE RESPECT CHART		
Duane	**Value**	**Marty**
1	1. I treat you with tenderness.	1
1	2. I submit my rights to you.	1
2	3. I open the car door for you.	3
1	4. We drop what we're doing and listen to each other.	1

CHART 10.1

List as many respect statements as you can (at least twenty). Together, come to an agreement on the three most important respect statements. If there are items that create conflict, talk about what you can do to resolve the conflict.

2. Share with each other what you presently do to show respect when you make love.

3. Discuss what each of you could do to show greater respect to the other in your lovemaking.

CHAPTER 10 Endnotes

1. Gary Smalley, *Love is a Decision* (Waco, Texas: Word Publishing, 1989), p. 21.

2. John Stott, *God's New Society* (Downers Grove, Illinois: InterVarsity Press, 1979), p. 232.

CHAPTER ELEVEN

Affair-Proofing Your Marriage

It was a hot, steamy night, and he saw her. Like a Peeping Tom, he saw her and wanted her. He knew enough people and pulled enough strings, and he found a way to frolic the night away with her in his bed. It made little difference that she was married, or that her faithful husband was off fighting—in his army. Only a one-night stand—he could get away with that, right?

Wrong. The seducer's lovely young bed partner got pregnant, and suddenly his whole political career was on the line. What did he do? He ordered the unknowing husband to return home. He imagined that after a night in bed, the soldier would assume the baby was his.

It didn't work that way.

The woman's husband was a man of principle. He didn't understand why his commanding officer had brought him home, but he determined that if his buddies were still out on the battlefield, dying like flies, he wasn't going to betray their cause by making love to his wife. He slept alone.

His C.O. was in a real bind now. He reassigned the soldier. "I've got a special job for you. Here are your sealed orders. Give them to your captain." The sealed orders contained the C.O.'s solution to the problem: murder.

I wonder what the innocent husband must have thought when his comrades were abruptly pulled away from the battlefront and, without warning, the enemy cut him down?

First adultery. Then murder. Then the death of the child conceived in this ungodly union, followed by political turmoil. You know how the scenario played out. It's in the Bible—the true story of David and Bathsheba. This couple's affair wasn't an isolated historical incident, as you know—adultery is rampant today.

SHOCKING BUT TRUE

Did you know every marriage has the potential for adultery? That may not seem like a particularly romantic notion, but it's absolutely true. Of course, we shouldn't spend our lives worrying about the threat of unfaithfulness. Instead, we should focus on building a wonderful relationship with our spouse. Still, let's be alert to the dangers.

God warns us,

> Do not lust in your heart after her beauty [the immoral woman] or let her captivate you with her eyes, for the prostitute reduces you to a loaf of bread, and the adulteress preys upon your very life. Can a man scoop fire into

his lap without his clothes being burned? Can a man walk on hot coals without his feet being scorched? So is he who sleeps with another man's wife; no one who touches her will go unpunished (Proverbs 6:25-29, NIV).

One of the devastating effects of sexual sin is that it is so very hard to overcome. The writer of Proverbs states it this way, "The evil deeds of a wicked man ensnare him; the cords of his sin hold him fast. He will die for lack of discipline, led astray by his own great folly" (Proverbs 5:22-23, NIV).

How widespread is this devastation? Miriam Horn, in an article in *U.S. News and World Report*, claimed that at least one third of married men and women are having or have had an affair lasting an average of one year.[1] Couple that with a 1988 survey done by sociologist Annette Lawson, which showed that sixty-six percent of her survey group had been unfaithful.[2]

Is it any wonder there are so many divorces, so much pain and suffering, so many unhappy people? America has been having an affair with lust for nearly thirty years, ever since the Sexual Revolution began.

SEX IS A CULTURAL CONCERN

Sex has become America's favorite idol, misleading us into sexual bondage rather than granting deliverance. Turn on the television or go to the movies and you will see every imaginable kind of sexual activity taking place, without concern for marriage, morality, or personal integrity. Listen to the radio, and you'll hear lyrics that glorify casual and extramarital sex. Take a walk in the shopping mall and browse around in some bookstores—you will discover that the covers of many books are suggestive and seductive. And the text between those inviting covers is often focused on illicit relationships, sexual perversion, and promiscuity.

What you are seeing all around you is also reflected in many of our churches. In a *U.S. News and World Report* article, author Jeffery Sheler writes about the declining membership in mainline Protestant church denominations. That decline has drawn leaders to debate about whether the church is relevant or if it is out of touch with cultural norms, impeding its ability to minister to people's needs.

Has the church been too strict in its view of sexuality by limiting sex to marriage? A task force was appointed by church leaders *to decide whether illicit relationships are responsible, the dynamics genuinely mutual, and the loving full of joyful caring.*[3]

In a *Time* magazine article, author Richard Ostling points out that Presbyterians, Episcopalians, Methodists, Roman Catholics, American Baptists, and others are wrestling with their understandings about sex from the Scriptures. Are these ideas simply cultural expressions? Some leaders are even telling us that modern reality assaults the belief that sex should be confined to marriage, and judgment on "sexual" activity should be based on the relative value of each relationship.[4]

GOD'S PURPOSES FOR MARRIAGE

I think we all agree that our marriages are of immense value, but what is God's intention for holy matrimony? Let's consider His purposes for marriage, as revealed in His Word.

PURPOSE #1—MARRIAGE IS FOR PROPAGATION.

Genesis 1:28 reminds us, "Be fruitful and increase in number." One of the joyous privileges a married couple has is to cooperate with God in an act ordained by Him to bring children into being.

PURPOSE #2—MARRIAGE IS FOR PLEASURE.

"The Lord God said, 'It is not good for man to be alone. I will make a helper suitable for him' " (Genesis 2:18, NIV). Pair by pair, God presented all the animals and birds before Adam to be named by him—they were male and female, to complement each other. Adam could see that they enjoyed each other. But for Adam, the Scripture reveals, "no suitable helper was found." Then God created a woman for the man to complement him.

Now there was a counterpart, one of man's own kind but yet *different*—one who would help Adam, one who would walk beside him, one who would lie down beside him, one who would receive him into herself and bear their children. They would become one flesh; not just sexually, but a mental and spiritual oneness was to develop, as well.

PURPOSE #3—MARRIAGE IS PREVENTION.

Here's what Paul wrote to the Corinthian church:

> Now for the matters you wrote about: It is good for a man not to marry. But since there is so much immorality, each man should have his own wife, and each woman her own husband. The husband should fulfill his marital duty to his wife, and likewise the wife to her husband. The wife's body does not belong to her alone but also to her husband. In the same way, the husband's body does not belong to him alone but also to his wife.
>
> Do not deprive each other except by mutual consent and for a time, so that you may devote yourselves to prayer. Then come together again so that Satan will not tempt you because of your lack of self-control. I say this as a concession, not as a command. I wish that all men were as I am. But each man has his own gift from God; one has this gift, another has that (1 Corinthians 7:1-7, NIV).

I don't believe this passage is teaching that celibacy is a more desirable situation than marriage. Later in chapter seven, it appears Paul states that the Corinthians are undergoing persecution. Rather than becoming a widow or widower before the honeymoon is over, it might be better to remain single. But, to avoid immorality, it would be best to marry. Marriage is the means of preventing immorality.

Paul's premise was that sex, outside of marriage, perverts God's design for marriage. Sex is more than a physical act. It joins two people together, and when sex occurs outside of marriage, a person sins against himself. Our bodies are the temple of the Holy Spirit of God. Sex within marriage has been ordained by God; outside of marriage, it is a sin against God. It devastates lives.

PRINCIPLES TO LIVE BY

Is adultery so rampant that no faithful spouses are left in America? Don't believe this for a moment. If in one third of marriages one spouse has cheated, then in two thirds of marriages spouses have not cheated. Not everyone is doing it. Not everyone is having an affair; nor do you ever need to look for greener grass when you can discover the green, green grass of home. Charlie and Martha Shedd, in *Celebration in the Bedroom*, encourage us with our first principle for keeping our marriages safe.

PRINCIPLE #1—WE DO NOT TAKE OUR STANDARDS FROM THE WORLD AROUND US.

What if everybody *is* doing it? As followers of the Lord, we are called to live with an eye single to glory. We should not take our standards from the world around us.[5]

Always, our call comes from the Highest Source. This call is a call to faithfulness, a call for men and women to make a commitment to be biblical in their viewpoint about marriage and sex. The world around you, the place you work, and the material you read cannot be allowed to dictate your standards. You must measure the ideas and values by the Highest Standard of all—God's Word.

PRINCIPLE #2—WE WILL BE FENCE BUILDERS.

Years ago, someone told me that if I really wanted to experience joy and fulfillment I should start building fences. Building fences? I didn't understand the concept until it was explained that the very first fence should be constructed around my marriage. Here's how this works. The four sides of the marital fence are Faithfulness, Respect, Honesty, and Love.

There are no gates. I can't get out, but neither can my spouse. And the boundaries not only keep us in, they keep the standards of the world outside. When things are rough, we don't try to escape; we let the boundaries protect us. Rather than inhibit our freedom, the fence provides a safe area within which we can express freedom together.

PRINCIPLE #3—WE WILL CONFINE SEX TO MARRIAGE.

It should be unnecessary to even mention this principle, but since Christians are so frequently involved in affairs, it bears repeating. Furthermore, figures state that over fifty percent of Christian young people believe premarital sex is all right, as long as love and only one partner are involved.

God's attitude about our sexual lives is that, "Marriage should be honored by all, and the marriage bed kept pure" (Hebrews 13:4, NIV). Marriage, in this context, is probably a euphemism for "sexual intercourse." Whether God is speaking of the marriage institution or sexual intercourse, the truths are the same. How do you honor your marriage? Here are four key ways:

- ***Remember the vow you once took.*** "I promise to forsake all others and keep myself only to her/him, as long as I live." What did you say? You said, "I will be faithful to you and you alone."

- ***Pray over your marriage bed.*** Together, pray about your sex life. Ask God to help you live in such a way that you look forward to sleeping with each other and making love. Ask God to help you improve your sex life, and to help you make it more than just exciting sex, but an extension of a life shared in oneness.

- ***Thank God that your spouse wants you.*** Develop habits and attitudes that foster desirability. You don't have to be Tom Cruise or Cindy Crawford to be exciting. Cleanliness, neatness, appropriate words, and positive attitudes go a long way toward making you a desirable person.

- ***Be a servant.*** "My partner doesn't meet my needs anymore" is a cry heard in counseling sessions from coast to coast. First of all, are you communicating your needs? Avoid grumbling, "If he (or she) loved me, he'd know what I need without being told!" That's unfair. Spouses aren't mind-readers, and that sort of thinking leads to resentment and bitterness.

However, if you've expressed your needs, and your spouse is unable to respond for one reason or another, you can choose to give anyway. You can demonstrate a servant's heart by meeting your partner's needs even when your own needs aren't being met. When you choose to give without receiving, do so cheerfully, generously, and with patience.

Why is it important to understand God's purposes and to honor certain principles in marriage? Fences, boundaries and principles are like gravity. If you ignore them, you may find yourself taking a sudden crash course in marital disaster. But if you honor them, you are free to move about, any way you please, within their clear and protective parameters. You'll be safe and sane. And you'll never be sorry.

OPPORTUNITIES FOR GROWTH

1. If you know of a marriage devastated by infidelity, discuss the consequences of this together. How is your marriage different from that marriage? In what ways is it similar? List two actions the two of you will take to strengthen your marriage.

2. Discuss your TV-viewing habits. Do you watch unwholesome shows? How about unwholesome movies? How do such shows and movies affect the thoughts and emotions of each of you? How do they impact your sexual life? Be honest. List some specific steps you will take to change any unhealthy viewing habits.

3. Using the fence-builder model, talk about how taking the "fence" position will strengthen your marriage.

4. Talk together about why your principles for marriage should be different from society's permissive "standards."

CHAPTER 11 Endnotes

1 Miriam Horn, "Goings on Behind Bedroom Doors," *U.S. News and World Report*, June 10, 1991, p. 64.

2. Ibid.

3. Jeffery Sheler, "The Gospel On Sex," *U.S. News and World Report*, June 10, 1991, pp. 55-61.

4. Richard Ostling, "What Does God Really Think about Sex?", *Time*, January 24, 1991, p. 48.

5. Charlie and Martha Shedd, *Celebration in the Bedroom* (Dallas, Texas: Word Books, 1979), p. 40.

CHAPTER TWELVE

Encouragement and Togetherness

In our busy local grocery store, I ran into a friend of Marty's. "Marty sure is proud of you!" she told me during the conversation. Although she went on to explain, I didn't need to know why. My heart was moved, no matter what. I know one thing—my wife is the president of my fan club. And that day, as I drove home, my feelings for Marty were warm and grateful.

I especially appreciate Marty's ongoing encouragement after listening to so many unpleasant statements from other husbands and wives. I've counseled hundreds of couples, and it never fails to sadden me when I realize that the majority of them have fallen into the trap of speaking negatively about their partners. They've become insulting. Sometimes their words are abusive. They're incredibly quick to let me know what they don't like about their spouse, but when I ask them to share what they do like, they instantly develop laryngitis.

Of course, this doesn't mean couples should neglect speaking about difficulties, needs, or problems. It *does* mean we should deal with problems in a loving, healing way. When faced with a difficult situation, we can ask each other:

- *How can we benefit from this situation?*
- *How should we deal with the situation in a positive way?*
- *How can we use this to strengthen our marriage?*
- *What can we do or say to alleviate one another's fears, allowing us to communicate openly and honestly?*
- *How can we encourage each other?*

That last option is a wonderful question, and a key to marital harmony. How can we encourage each other? Words are profoundly important, and kind words are a good place to begin. But encouragement involves far more than words. As the cynic sometimes says, "Yeah, right. Talk is cheap." How can we encourage our spouses through actions? Here are some suggestions I've gleaned from my counseling files:

ACTION STEP 1—EXPRESS LOVE.

Love is expressed in kind acts which demonstrate your feelings. A phone call during the day. Flowers. A thoughtful card. A dinner out. An unexpected present. And don't overlook that much-appreciated question: "What can I do to help?"

ACTION STEP 2—NURTURE YOUR LOVE RELATIONSHIP.

Remember that marital garden we talked about before? Nurturing requires tending, pruning, and feeding. One significant way to care for your love relationship is to attend marriage seminars with the purpose of discovering ways to meet each other's needs.

You may choose to read books together. Discuss each chapter as you go, and if there are assignments, do them jointly. The idea is not just to learn new principles, but to be united, to do something as a couple.

I know a husband and wife who routinely visit a marriage counselor annually to have a marriage "checkup." The questions they are asked help them focus on areas where they can continue to grow.

ACTION STEP 3—COOPERATE WITH EACH OTHER.

It's amazing. Before couples are married, they tend to spend all their time with each other, yet after marriage they often take each other for granted. Far too often they go in separate directions, and find themselves irritated by the very things they enjoyed when they were dating. Cooperating means working through the challenges, taking the bad with the good, and learning to say, "I love you just the way you are."

ACTION STEP 4—OBSERVE.

Be on the lookout for ways to creatively demonstrate love. One man's wife had an old pickup truck she loved to drive. The tail lights didn't work, and she was unable to drive it at night. They didn't have the funds to fix it. His wife periodically mentioned that it would be nice to have the lights fixed.

I know this man well, and what he knows about fixing a vehicle would fit in a thimble; but he wanted to fix the tail lights. He saved enough money to buy the necessary wiring, got a friend to assist him, and fixed the lights. He didn't tell his wife what he had done. After she noticed they were working, she ran to her husband when he got home, hugged him around the neck, and exclaimed, "You fixed the truck! You did it [it sounded like she thought it was a miracle; maybe it was]. You fixed the truck! You really do love me. Thank you!"

ACTION STEP 5—UNDERSTAND, DON'T LECTURE.

Men often think women want solutions, when they really long to be heard and comforted. Women sometimes moralize and try to superimpose "life lessons" upon men's struggles. Efforts to simply listen, care, and understand will be met with improved communication and greater openness.

ACTION STEP 6—REMEMBER TO SHARE PAST BLESSINGS FOR WHICH YOU ARE THANKFUL.

Remember the events that drew you close to each other. This is so important. Share memories, and pray together in praise, as well as in need.

ACTION STEP 7—ACCEPT EACH OTHER'S STRENGTHS AND WEAKNESSES.

How often do we have to remind ourselves, "Nobody's perfect"? Marriages are marred by "if only…" thinking that refuses to allow for idiosyncrasies. "I love you—just the way you are" is an incredibly freeing statement.

ACTION STEP 8—GIVE YOUR LOVE UNCONDITIONALLY.

If you're anything like me, defining "unconditional love" is difficult. Picture, then, what it means to place conditions on marital love. Unconditional love is the opposite. Jesus Christ is the only One who truly loves unconditionally, but unconditional love should be our goal. It's in the incubator of unconditional love where change and growth are born.

ACTION STEP 9—ENJOY EACH OTHER.

Enjoyment means seeking togetherness and finding common interests. We'll talk more about this important step in the pages that follow. Meanwhile, if you forget how to demonstrate your love, review this simple acrostic (E-N-C-O-U-R-A-G-E):

Express love.

Nurture your relationship.

Cooperate with each other.

Observe ways to creatively demonstrate love.

Understand, don't lecture.

Remember your blessings.

Accept each other.

Grow together.

Enjoy each other.

A CELEBRATION OF ACCEPTANCE

Please notice the inclusion of mutual acceptance in our ENCOURAGE acrostic above. Acceptance plays a vital role in marital joy and togetherness. In fact, it is of foundational importance in developing and maintaining a loving marital relationship. I'd like to show you how you and your spouse can *celebrate* acceptance.

I look for opportunities to celebrate. Not just birthdays, anniversaries, Christmas, and so on...I celebrate when I'm awestruck by a beautiful waterfall or a rainbow on a stormy day;

when I experience children laughing; when I see a pony prance through a pasture in the spring. All these are reasons for me to celebrate. So developing a Celebration of Acceptance was easy for Marty and me.

Celebrate means "to demonstrate satisfaction in someone or something by festivities or some other deviation from routine." *Acceptance* means "the act of showing approval."

GOD'S EXAMPLE

This is God's declaration: "Accept one another, then, just as Christ accepted you, in order to bring praise to God" (Romans 15:7, NIV). Since Christ brought praise to God by accepting us, we can bring praise to God by accepting our mates.

We often have an easier time accepting people we barely know than the people closest to us. This may be due to the good first impression strangers are trying to make. We see their strengths—whereas, in the case of our partners, we often focus more on weaknesses. Unfortunately, the very people who most need our approval and acceptance often go without it. A commitment to accept your partner is necessary for intimacy. A celebration of acceptance is a beautiful and unique way to let your partner know you accept him or her. Let's look at what form this observance might take in *my* home.

It's the day of our celebration, and we've just finished a romantic dinner. We begin by discussing each other's strengths. I may say, "Marty, you're wonderful at developing one-to-one relationships. You're calm, easygoing, diplomatic, conservative, and a wonderful team player. I believe we make a great team. You're patient with me when I jump from activity to activity. You're patient with the grandkids when they demand attention, too. I praise God that you're so family-oriented and don't get upset with others easily. These are some of your strengths, and I accept them. I affirm these in you."

She shares a similar list with me.

Next, we point out talents, skills, abilities, and things the other did well during the past month. Marty lets me know she is amazed I can handle multiple projects as well as I do. She adds, "Duane, you're a talented speaker. Your series of messages at the Bible conference were so practical; especially the one when you shared how to develop a mission statement for marriage."

Then we talk about character qualities we've noticed in each other recently. Marty points out the quality of dependability in my life. I mention how her loyalty touches me deeply.

Before you conclude your *own* celebration, if you're experiencing a difficulty or problem in your marriage, make a commitment together to work through it. Don't dwell on the problem, but mutually express your willingness to work at resolving it.

As you discuss any difficulties, share your awareness of your own weaknesses. Admit them openly. Weaknesses are not sins;

they are opportunities to trust God. For example, I can get so involved with people that I forget tasks. In this area, I have an opportunity to trust God for time management. Marty complements me in this area with her attention to details. Let your partner know how beautifully he or she fills in what is lacking in your life.

A DECLARATION OF ACCEPTANCE

Conclude your celebration with a declaration of acceptance. The Epistle of James tells us, "Every good and perfect gift is from above, coming down from the Father" (James 1:17, NIV). Your spouse is a gift, given for your good. Verbally accept him or her as a gift from God. Make sure you are facing each other and making eye contact as each of you, in turn, declares...

> "I accept you, ____________________ (spouse's name), as a gift from God to help me become more like Jesus Christ. I accept your strengths and your weaknesses. You are made in the image of God, and I value you. I will not seek to change you but will change only myself. I will complement you so that we will be more 'one' spiritually, emotionally, and physically. Thank you for being my gift. I love you because I choose to love you, and I love you because of who you are."

An acceptance vow such as this, when repeated from time to time over the years, will give you a new appreciation for the one you married. It will remind you of your commitment to each other.

Before you go to bed, kneel together and pray. Pray for your mate. Pray for growing acceptance. Praise God aloud for the wonderful blessing your mate is in your life.

MARRIAGE MISSION STATEMENT

Another wonderful means of encouraging your spouse is to develop a *marriage mission statement* together. The restlessness and despair in our society has long been associated with purposelessness. People often ask, "Why am I here?" The same inquiry can be made about personal projects and relationships. The answer is something we call "mission." Why not formally affirm the things that are important to each of you? Stephen Covey states in *The 7 Habits of Highly Effective People,* "The core of any family is what is changeless, what is always going to be there."[1]

FOUR GUIDING PRINCIPLES

When you put your mission statement together, include both principles and expectations. Here are four guiding principles for marriage. As you develop your own mission you may want to include others.

1. We will *LOVE* each other intentionally and unconditionally.
2. We will *RESPECT* each other.

3. We will be *HONEST* with each other.

4. We will be *FAITHFUL* to each other.

FOUR KEY EXPECTATIONS

You may want to add your own concerns to this list of four key expectations:

1. We expect each to value the other's opinions and input into decisions.

2. We expect to be treated and to treat the other with dignity.

3. We expect each to contribute to the other's well-being.

4. We expect to make a contribution about life to our children, grandchildren, and our friends.

Talk about the things that matter most to you and your spouse—discuss them, write them out, rewrite them, and prioritize them. And don't be in a hurry. It can take a corporation over six months to develop a mission statement. As the process continues, however, employees draw closer to each other. They begin to share more of their lives with one another. That's exactly what should happen in a marriage. This process of developing a mission will help you develop closeness. Your mission statement may sound something like this:

The mission of our marriage is to glorify God by developing oneness, displaying Christlike character qualities, and by demonstrating the love of Jesus Christ to each other and to all those we come in contact with.

TOGETHERNESS AND COMMON INTERESTS

A tremendous sense of encouragement inspires us as we work together toward common goals. And besides goals, it is also encouraging to develop other common interests and projects with our spouses. People naturally delight in the experience of "togetherness" that comes from sharing mutual activities.

Of course, togetherness is more than just being in the same house or the same room. In a culture that has been anesthetized by television, a couple can spend countless hours watching TV and never communicate. Add that to being apart while one or both are working, spending time with the children, and church activities. It's easy to spend twenty-five years together and finally look up and say, "Hello. Do I know you?" In a hectic world like ours, togetherness clearly doesn't happen automatically.

Look at it this way—if it takes fifteen hours a week to romance your mate before marriage, it takes the same amount of time after the vows are exchanged. An impossible task? Maybe. But togetherness is enhanced when couples establish common interests. What are you willing to do together? The chart on the next page provides a starter list of ideas.

THINGS TO DO TOGETHER		
1. Attend concerts	31. Reading	61. Hospital volunteer work
2. Attend movies	32. Go to art museums	62. Tutoring
3. Attend ball games	33. Go to history museums	63. Bible studies
4. Attend church socials	34. Go to science museums	64. Attend lectures (your interest)
5. Attend dramas	35. Rollerblading	65. Hot-air ballooning
6. Bicycle riding	36. Picnicking	66. Cake decorating
7. Rock climbing	37. Sight-seeing	67. Badminton
8. Skiing	38. Shopping	68. Croquet
9. Tennis	39. Bible reading	69. Ping-pong
10. Golfing	40. Collect antiques	70. Whale watching
11. Swimming	41. Bus touring	71. Bird watching
12. Collect sea shells	42. Train touring	72. Garage sales
13. Scuba dive	43. Kite flying	73. Remodeling houses
14. Horseback riding	44. Learn a foreign language	74. Keep a family journal
15. Attend state or county fairs	45. Exercise	75. Take an art class
16. Attend craft or hobby shows	46. Bowling	76. Attend auctions
17. Jog	47. Square dancing	77. Quilting
18. Play board or card games	48. Politics	78. Jewelry making
19. Camping	49. Civic meetings	79. Sculpturing
20. Fishing	50. P.T.A.	80. Join a conservation club
21. Hiking	51. Furniture refinishing	81. Care for a pet
22. Gardening	52. Stamp collecting	82. Record and tape collecting
23. Landscaping	53. Coin collecting	83. Listening to music
24. Painting	54. Astronomy	84. Join a drama group
25. Take a college class together	55. Teach a class	85. Speaking
26. Photography	56. Youth work	86. Join a service club
27. Snowmobiling	57. Ceramics	87. Mission tours
28. Ice-skating	58. Co-ed sports team	88. Flying
29. Boating	59. Pool	89. Trail-biking
30. Cooking	60. Start a small business	90. Play musical instruments

CHART 12.1

HOW DO WE KNOW WHEN WE'RE HAVING FUN?

If one purpose of developing common interests is to communicate with each other, there is certainly another purpose of equal importance: having fun. Over the years, I've observed that couples who are going through difficulties have stopped having fun together. The proverb that says "couples who pray together, stay together" has been hanging around for a long time. I would take it a step further:

COUPLES WHO PRAY
AND PLAY TOGETHER,
STAY TOGETHER.

Somehow, the puritanical concept that if it is pleasurable it must be wrong, has subtly cemented itself to contemporary Christianity. Somewhere between childhood and adulthood, we have come to believe that pleasure ends, and we must become responsible sufferers. Granted, there is a living to make, children to raise, problems to solve, and wounds to be bandaged, but where in the world does it say fun is finished for married couples? The preacher in Ecclesiastes, sharing that there was a time and season for everything, commented that there is "a time to weep and a time to laugh, a time to mourn and a time to dance" (Ecclesiastes 3:4, NIV).

How do you know when you're having fun? Are you enjoying each other as well as what you're doing? Are you frolicking hand in hand? Ask yourself how much you laugh together. Do you ever laugh with each other when you're making love?

SEX—THE ULTIMATE IN TOGETHERNESS

Sex is relational, and like conversation, lovemaking takes time. Why not make a date for sexual intimacy once a week? Decide which evening it will be in advance—how many hours or days in advance is up to you. Schedule part of your day to be free of any work or activities. Speak to each other in loving anticipation throughout the course of the day. When the time arrives, embrace each other. Undress each other. Go to bed early, naked.

In bed, explore each other's bodies. Talk about your sexual feelings as you hold each other. Some men may have difficulty talking during foreplay and sexual intercourse, but it's worth the effort. Express how you feel about each other. Direct your partner toward arousal spots. Even though one of you may be highly aroused, wait until the other is ready for intercourse. Talk with each other.

When you have both reached an orgasm, hold and kiss each other, and don't be in a hurry to turn over and go to sleep. Talk about what you are experiencing and what caused you enjoyment. Take all the time in the world to delight in the pleasure of being together. And be encouraged—you're experiencing the greatest intimacy and togetherness possible between two people. It is God's gift to you—and your gift to each other.

Good night. I'm sure you'll sleep well.

OPPORTUNITIES FOR GROWTH

1. Set a date to have a Celebration of Acceptance, and enjoy each other.

2. Develop a mission statement for your marriage. You might include these elements: • the strengths of your marriage • the principles which guide your marriage • the way the two of you view your roles • your expectations of each other • your family values. Don't be in a hurry. You may want to spend several hours over several weeks. Begin your mission statement with: *The purpose of our marriage is to…*

3. Keep a journal for the next six months of the time you spend together. Keep track of: • how much time you spend together each week • what you can do to better use your time together.

4. Take sixty minutes and list your common interests and activities. What does your list reveal to you? Discuss common interests and activities that you would like to share together. Develop a plan to research and explore a *new* interest or activity together.

5. Discuss the idea that love takes time. Explore how you can set special evenings aside to make love.

CHAPTER 12 Endnote

1. Stephen R. Covey, *The 7 Habits of Highly Effective People* (New York, New York: Simon and Schuster, 1989), p. 138.

RESOURCES AVAILABLE

Personality System

Biblical Personality System

Values Assessment

To order the above materials or to inquire about other resources and seminars, contact:

Sanford Kulkin
Institute for Motivational Living
1-800-779-3472

Or:

Duane L. Storey
Resources for Communication Concepts
P.O. Box 1124
Sisters, OR 97759
1-503-549-1124

Or (for seminars and speaking engagements):

Mary Ann Mayo
A Woman's Place Medical Center
652 Petaluma Ave., Suite A
Sebastopol, CA 95472
1-707-823-8811